Serial Killers

The Horrific True Crime Stories Behind

4 Infamous Serial Killers

That Shocked the World

Real Crime By Real Killers Collection 1

Ryan Becker, True Crime Seven

TRUE CRIME 7

ISBN: 978-1089520344

Table of Contents

Explore the Stories of

The Murderous Minds

A Note

From True Crime Seven

Hi there!

Thank you so much for picking up our book! Before you continue your exploration into the dark world of killers, we wanted to take a quick moment to explain the purpose of our books.

Our goal is to simply explore and tell the stories of various killers in the world: from unknown murderers to infamous serial killers. Our books are designed to be short and inclusive; we want to tell a good scary true story that anyone can enjoy regardless of their reading level.

That is why you won't see too many fancy words or complicated sentence structures in our books. Also, to prevent the typical cut and dry style of true crime books, we try to keep the narrative easy to follow while incorporating fiction style storytelling. As to information, we often find ourselves with too little or too much. So, in terms of research material and content, we always try to include what further helps the story of the killer.

Lastly, we want to acknowledge that, much like history, true crime is a subject that can often be interpreted differently. Depending on the topic and your upbringing, you might agree or disagree with how we present a story. We understand disagreements are inevitable. That is why we added this note so hopefully, it can help you better understand our position and goal.

Now without further ado, let the exploration to the dark begin!

Robert Berdella

The True Story of a Man Who Turned His Darkest Fantasies into A Reality

Introduction

SOMETHING MUST BE SAID: WE ARE FORTUNATE.

We are fortunate because we can sit in the safety of our homes and pick up books like these as a source of entertainment and knowledge, distractions of sorts that allow us to learn the tales of horrible human beings. We are fortunate because as soon as we put these books down, we simply push the horrific details to the back of our minds and or let them remain on the pages of said books. Soon, we forget about them or replace them with more pleasant information.

The victims of the killers we describe, however, are not so fortunate.

Everyone in the world has dreams, desires, and fantasies. While some may wish to travel or possess riches, others may have fantasies of a more intimate nature. There is no real problem with desiring that which you cannot easily have, with wishing for something that may be out of your reach.

Unfortunately, some desires are of the deepest, darkest kind.

A serial killer is described by the Federal Bureau of Investigation as: 'an offender who commits a series of two or more murders in separate events, usually, but not always, acting alone.' Most killers are troubled beings who suffered traumatic childhoods and cannot live normal, decent lives without causing damage to those around them; others simply enjoy the rush of killing without being discovered. There are many, many more reasons for a human to stray into the act of serial killing, but an even worse category of killer awaits us—one which includes the particular subject of this tale.

Sick individuals have always plagued humanity—monsters that have lost all empathy for their fellow humans and cannot see past their own personal desires. These include the murderous dictators of recent, as well as those long-dead in the past, the leaders of organizations who have taken lives for perverted or unforgivable reasons such as political or racial preferences, and finally those particular beasts disguised by human flesh that have seen fit to experiment on their own species as if they were cattle.

The subject of this book is one such figure who fits into the latter group.

The press named him *The Butcher of Kansas City*. He was a true psychopath who sadistically tortured and killed at least six men during a three-year period. However, until he confessed and was arrested, our killer was known simply as Robert Berdella.

Robert was a quiet, intelligent fellow, who—besides being appreciated by his neighbors as a civic-minded individual—was also a great lover of art, cooking, and different cultures. His activities ranged from hobbies as innocent as stamp collecting to more incriminating pursuits such as possession of illegal drugs and experimentation on animals.

Even so, these particular activities gave no indication of what Berdella would later become. Perhaps one thing led to another, but in truth, it seems more likely that he finally let go of his decency and embraced an evil that had long lingered within his mind.

The murders were ugly events, but it was what Berdella did to his victims *before* death that horrified the entire nation. He experimented on his victims, causing terrible damage to their organs and bodies in general, and usually kept them captive for weeks before they died. Injections of chemical substances, electric shocks, rape, and insertion of objects were just a few of the activities that took place within Berdella's home. It most definitely can be said that *The Butcher of Kansas City* deserved his nickname.

In the following book, we will relive the tale of this sadistic individual—a man who happily confessed his crimes once caught and talked about having been influenced by *The Collector*, a 1965 movie that allowed him to 'make some of his darkest fantasies become a reality,' as he said at the time.

This book will tell the story of *The Butcher of Kansas City* from his origins to his end.

Do not believe for one second that the grisly details of Berdella's murders shall be censored or kept from you; these details have been preserved through time thanks to Berdella's own Polaroids and diary. You need to be prepared, beloved reader…

…you're in for a gruesome recount.

I

A God-Fearing Boy

OUR STORY BEGINS IN CUYAHOGA FALLS, OHIO, on the 31st of January, 1949. Robert Andrew Berdella, Jr. was born to Robert Sr. and Alice Berdella, a practicing Catholic couple who immediately integrated their new son into their faith. Robert's younger brother, Daniel, was born when Robert was seven, and the two were raised as good, well-behaved boys who avoided bad behavior, lest they anger their strict father.

The young Robert suffered a large amount of bullying during his childhood years due to his nearsightedness that required him to wear thick glasses. He slowly turned in to a loner who rarely got involved in group activities or social interaction with friends. He was a good student with decent grades, but the constant bullying marred his school years and created a distant boy who behaved in a detached manner

Berdella's teenage years were heavily influenced by his disaffection with Catholicism and a life-changing discovery: he was a homosexual.

When Robert was just sixteen, his father died of a heart attack at thirty-nine years of age. This caused great sadness in the boy, but nothing hurt him more than when his mother remarried and moved in with the man just a few months later. In Robert's immature mind, this was enough reason to feel insanely angry—he felt as though his mother had flippantly discarded his father's memory and grabbed a new lover instantly, while he himself was still grieving.

Initially, Robert attempted to find solace in religion, but this became harder every day, as the pain of losing his father ate away at him. This, along with an incident at work when a male co-worker took advantage and sexually abused Robert, made him reconsider his faith, and he abandoned the Catholic Church for good. He developed a cynical attitude toward religion and began to read and investigate different faiths, without truly believing in any of them.

Around the time of his father's death in 1965, Robert watched the film adaptation of the book, *The Collector*. He saw the protagonist capture a beautiful woman, hold her captive in an underground, windowless room, and study her as a sort of specimen. The movie left an impression on the young Berdella, one that was strong enough for him to decide eventually to recreate these events in real life.

Berdella graduated from high school in the summer of 1967. Before long, he moved to Kansas City for a change of scenery. He wanted to study art and become a professor at the Kansas City Art Institute. In college, Berdella was considered to be a talented student who worked extra hard at finding inspiration. However, he worked equally hard at abusing alcohol, and he even began to sell minor drugs to addicted classmates. This eventually came back to bite him when he was picked up by the police for possession of drugs. Luckily for Berdella, they lacked sufficient evidence to impose anything harsher than a fine.

Although Berdella had friends in college, he still lacked the mercy that many normal human beings possess. On three particular occasions, Berdella experimented on live animals during art classes; the final time he murdered a dog in front of a crowd 'for art.' The College Board decided that enough was enough. Berdella was stripped of his place at the Kansas City Art Institute, an occurrence that caused him a significant amount of shame.

Where a normal person may have taken this as a signal to turn their life around, Berdella felt aggrieved by his expulsion from the Institute. Surely the Board at the Center of Studies simply didn't understand his brand of art and were *clearly* just repressing his desires. It was at this moment the young Berdella, already troubled, took a turn for the worse.

For the much, much worse, in fact.

II

Berdella's Bizarre Bazaar

DURING HIS TIME STUDYING ART, ROBERT HAD adopted some unusual pastimes, such as collecting oddities and writing to distant pen pals in countries such as Vietnam and Burma. His interest in primitive art and antiques would eventually drive his desire to open a business in this field, but first, he needed to earn the necessary funds.

Thus, in 1969, following his expulsion from the Kansas City Art Institute, Berdella changed his direction in life. After brief consideration, he decided to move to the Hyde Park district of Kansas City. There, he was a helpful neighbor within the community, taking part in Crime Prevention and Neighborhood

Watch patrols, and gaining the love and respect of his fellow Hyde Park residents. He was also known for participating in fundraising events for a local television station.

Another more secret, yet equally respectable side of Robert's life, was what he did for several vulnerable young men of the city in the early 70s. After having a brief relationship with a Vietnam War veteran, Berdella began spending time with young males who had gotten into prostitution, drugs, or had run away. He tried his hardest to steer these young men back on to the right track and assist them in leaving their harmful lifestyles behind. Those that were unaware of the sexual nature of some of these relationships thought of Berdella as a sort of 'foster parent' to these young men.

At the same time, Berdella attempted to improve himself on an interpersonal level, while he also strived to enhance his professionalism. Soon he started working as a cook throughout the city. When he wasn't working at a bar or restaurant, Robert found time to sell antique items and art to contacts, all from the comfort of his home. Both of these activities allowed him to succeed and cover his expenses—expenses of which he would soon have many, including lawyer fees and fines that accumulated due to arrests. Berdella eventually became a prestigious, well-known cook in town, working for renowned businesses and even joining a chefs' association where he helped train young students at a local culinary college.

Despite Berdella's success as a cook, however, he found his interest in antiques and oddities couldn't be denied, so he decided to invest the money he'd accumulated in starting an antique-selling business. In 1982, he rented a booth at the Westport Flea Market, naming it *Berdella's Bizarre Bazaar*. He sold jewelry and antiques to both curious amateurs and expert customers.

While managing the booth, Berdella befriended a man named Paul Howell, as well as his son, Jerry. Robert and Jerry soon formed a friendship. They were often seen sharing drinks in the company of friends. At other times, Berdella gave the young troublemaker a bit of legal advice.

To everyone around him, it looked like Robert had finally found someone to care about and spend time with—something he'd never truly had since childhood. What was happening in truth, however, was far more sinister.

Berdella was beginning to measure his first possible victim, a process that would end with bloodcurdling results.

III

The Bloodshed Commences

JERRY HOWELL WAS JUST NINETEEN WHEN IT happened. He'd owed Robert a sum of money for quite a while now and constantly evaded the man's questions whenever the issue came up. As time passed, he seemed less and less likely to pay the debt. This angered Berdella, who was already filled with strange and misguided anger—just waiting for a reason to unleash it on the world.

It didn't take long to manifest.

On July 4, 1984, Berdella decided he had waited long enough. The signs had been there for years, but nobody had paid attention. It wasn't really a killing instinct that drove Berdella, but rather the urge to cause pain and push the human body to its extremes. He felt he *needed* to know how much pain he could cause and how much damage and destruction he could inflict on a fellow man.

Berdella arrived at Jerry's home with an excuse already on his lips—he had come to take the young man to a dancing contest. Jerry, naïve of his friend's true motives, got in the car with Berdella. They drove for a while, with Berdella offering Jerry a drink in the car before they reached their destination. Unfortunately for Jerry, the drink was spiked with sedative drugs. Berdella simply drove around, killing time until Jerry no longer knew what was happening.

Berdella grew excited and took Jerry back home with him. He injected him with even more tranquilizer to keep him submissive. Berdella bred Chow-Chow dogs and had collected plenty of animal sedatives for when the perfect moment arose. The youth became unconscious, and all that Robert Berdella had ever hoped for was now his to enjoy: a helpless victim to torture as he saw fit.

He bound Jerry to his bed with glee, stripping him of his clothes and admiring his body—a body that became the target for more than twenty-four hours of sexual and physical abuse. Berdella didn't just rape Jerry personally during his horrific night of captivity; he also introduced foreign objects—such as a cucumber—into the youth's anus, tearing it without mercy.

Whenever Jerry was conscious enough to beg for mercy and ask Berdella why he was doing such terrible things, Berdella would answer with a quick shot of sedative, which put him back under. Berdella even went to work while the man was unconscious, an attempt to keep anyone from suspecting what was truly going on. *His plan worked.*

When he returned from work, Berdella had new ideas on how to cause agony to his captive's body. Taking advantage of the young man's helplessness, Berdella continued his torture despite Jerry's pleas for him to stop. The twisted torturer decided to keep mementos for his future pleasure and documented most of the process with his Polaroid camera and a notebook, a pair of items he would soon come to use very often.

The horrific ordeal ended only when young Jerry died sometime after midnight, July 5, 1984. Berdella would later confess that he was unsure whether it had been due to Jerry asphyxiating on his own vomit—he had been gagged for a long period of the torture—or the fact that the excess of medicines had stopped his breathing. After a brief and failed attempt at CPR, a disappointed

Berdella lifted up the now dead Jerry Howell and dragged him down to the basement.

There, he hung the corpse from the ceiling over a pot and climbed back upstairs to search for his set of cooking knives. Berdella worked on the victim's body like a butcher in a slaughterhouse, cutting open the jugular and inner elbow veins to drain the blood from the corpse.

Berdella left the body hanging overnight, returning the next morning to finish cutting it up with a chainsaw and bone knives. There was a feeling of dissatisfaction growing within him already, but he ignored it long enough to concentrate on disposing of the body in dog food bags that were then wrapped in larger black bags. The bags were left outside for the garbage collectors.

With his first victim dead, and a long and detailed document of the killing safely in his Polaroid pictures and diary, another killer may have called it a day.

Berdella, however, was just getting started.

IV

New Methods

AS WE HAVE ALREADY MENTIONED, ROBERT Berdella enjoyed helping young men get back on their feet during times of hardship. He allowed many of them to stay at his home until they could find jobs and piece their lives back together.

One such lodger was Robert Sheldon, a young man Berdella felt no attraction toward, but who was simply in the wrong place at the wrong time.

On April 10, 1985, Berdella heard a knock at his door. Suspicious, he went to see who had arrived at his home unannounced. Waiting at the door was twenty-three-year-old Sheldon, who needed a place to stay after having been evicted from his own home. Although Berdella agreed to take him in, something stirred within him.

It was a mix of discomfort at having someone living in his private space and a curious desire to try out more methods of pain—those he hadn't used in his first murder. He had anger and frustration bubbling within him. *What better way to unleash my feelings than on young Robert?*

So, on April 12, when Berdella arrived home from work to find Sheldon lying unconscious and intoxicated from having drunk too much, he allowed his darker side to manifest. Sheldon was too far gone to feel the needle that punctured his vein. The sedative rapidly spread through his body as Berdella prepared to torture his second victim.

It is interesting to note that, unlike with Jerry Howell, Berdella did not feel any kind of attraction toward Sheldon. This lack of sexual desire led him to avoid inflicting rape or any other type of sexual abuse on the twenty-three-year-old. This did not mean that Berdella was any less brutal in his methods.

He began by binding the young man and leading him up to the second-floor bedroom. There, he began the ordeal by waiting for Sheldon to return to consciousness before explaining what was about to happen to his captive. As the man reeled in shock, Berdella produced a syringe and proceeded to inject Drano—a well-known drain cleaner product—into Sheldon's eyes. Then he grabbed a metal rod and needles, alternating between forcefully smashing his victim's hands and inserting needles into his fingertips.

Berdella used caulking sealant in Sheldon's ears to keep him deaf and unaware of the sounds in his surroundings and raised the television volume to ensure his neighbors wouldn't be alerted by the victim's screams. He also bound Sheldon's wrists with piano wire, a sharp material that cut into the young man's nerves and tendons when he struggled, ensuring that, even if he survived, he'd never be able to use his hands properly again.

It didn't matter in the end

On April 15, three days after the torture began, a workman arrived at Berdella's home. The killer had forgotten he'd scheduled some roof work for that afternoon. Faced with discovery, Berdella quickly but reluctantly went up to the second floor, put a thick sack over Sheldon's head, and pulled a rope tight around the man's neck until he suffocated.

With Sheldon now dead, Berdella allowed the worker to enter his home. Once the worker had left, Berdella dragged the corpse to the third-floor bathroom and dissected it in the tub. Apart from Sheldon's head, he disposed of the corpse similarly to how he'd gotten rid of Howell. Then he sat down to read his notes and inspect his Polaroids. He had 'learned' plenty from both torture-murders. The pain he'd caused Sheldon had been quite intense, despite the fact that he'd left some of his plans unfinished due to the workman's interruption.

When night fell, Robert went out to the backyard with his victim's head. He buried it for safekeeping—similarly to the souvenirs he had at the Bizarre Bazaar —until when he would relocate it to a closet inside. Nobody had a clue.

Berdella was pretty sure of himself. *I could stop right now.* However, everything had been so easy, with nobody having any inkling of what he'd been doing. *Why stop, if nobody can catch me?*

Ultimately, this was what kept Berdella going—the fact that his victims' disappearances did not register or cause doubts within the community or among law enforcement. It was as if there were no consequences at all for what he had done. It felt as if he could keep going forever if he wanted to, and subsequently, he decided to continue killing.

To the misfortune of his victims, Berdella now felt *unstoppable.*

V

Hungry For More

JUNE CAME AND, WITH IT, A NEW VICTIM. BERDELLA had often hired the services of a youth named Mark Wallace, who did yard work in exchange for a bit of cash.

On one particular afternoon, as a severe thunderstorm raged overhead, Berdella looked out his window and spotted someone hiding in his shed. Squinting his eyes as he approached, he caught sight of Mark Wallace sheltering from the rain in there. Berdella was pleasant as always, calling the young man over and inviting him inside. While Mark believed that his employer's intentions were good, Berdella had already made up his mind.

Wallace would become his next victim.

As thunder and lightning tore through the sky outside, the two talked. Berdella noted the young man sitting across from him was feeling depressed and anxious. He offered him an injection of drugs, saying they would help him feel better and more relaxed. Mark was happy to accept. Berdella got a syringe full of chlorpromazine—a mild sedative—and injected it into the youth.

Unknowingly, Mark had just been manipulated into the worst situation he'd ever face.

Half an hour later, Berdella was carrying the unconscious Wallace up to the second-floor bedroom. Again, he waited for the young man to wake before commencing an entire day of pain and torture.

Berdella had recently been contemplating the effects of electrical shocks on the human body. He now had the chance to find out.

After attaching alligator clips to Wallace's nipples, he kept the youth awake and alert by shocking him whenever he seemed about to lose consciousness. He took photos and documented everything he did, eventually deciding to insert hypodermic needles into the young man's muscles. Berdella enjoyed the torture until Wallace suddenly stopped responding at seven p.m., June 23. He was dead.

Berdella cursed his luck and took the corpse to the bathroom upstairs, repeated his disposal procedure, and then took the black bags outside for the garbage crew to remove. As he watched the truck leaving with his victim's remains, Berdella was filled with certainty; a certainty he hadn't previously had.

He needed to keep killing until he was caught.

VI

A Full-Time Torturer

TO ROBERT BERDELLA, HIS ACTIONS WEREN'T just mindless torture and debauchery. On the contrary, in his mind, he was doing something worthwhile, something almost artistic or scientific: he was studying and experimenting on the human body like few ever had.

In reality, his desires were the reason for his actions, and Berdella was able to justify his actions by thinking of them in this way.

Only three months later, the next victim lay chained in Berdella's home. This time our killer wanted to escalate the severity of his methods.

On September 26, 1985, Berdella received a telephone call from a man known as Walter James Ferris, who had already spent time at his home on a previous occasion. Ferris wished to stay at Berdella's for a short period again, which Berdella found extremely convenient. His next victim had arrived, without him even looking for one.

In fact, Berdella would later admit that Ferris was the first man he'd taken home with the intention to torture, unlike his other three victims. In their cases, he had been unaware of what his true intentions were until they were within the walls of his house.

For this visit, Berdella and Walter met at a bar. They chatted and had a few drinks together before returning to Berdella's house. Once in the privacy of his home, Berdella immediately drugged Ferris with tranquilizers and tied him to his bed, where he would be tortured repeatedly for twenty-seven hours. His previous torture of Mark Wallace via electrical shocks had increased Berdella's appetite for this method of inducing pain. He soon began to subject the struggling Ferris to seven thousand seven hundred-volt shocks—both to his shoulders and testicles, each shock lasting as long as five minutes.

Berdella also continued where he'd left off with the hypodermic needles, ramming several into Ferris's neck and genitals, all while making notes in his diary. He made sure to document even the smallest details, studying the reaction caused by abuse to individual parts of the man's body.

Eventually, Berdella pushed Walter too hard; the man could no longer sit up or breathe properly. It seemed that Berdella had used an excessive amount of sedative. Consequently, Walter's breathing failed, and he died soon after. Berdella added a note in his diary indicating the end of another so-called 'project.'

Berdella felt contented with his studies, despite Ferris's untimely death. He rapidly dissected his victim's body in the upstairs bathroom, disposing of the corpse piece by piece into separate black bags. Again, the garbage crew ensured he remained undetected, and soon Berdella was back to living his normal life.

Months passed, and Berdella attempted to concentrate on his life. However, his desire to cause pain and study the human body through torture inevitably led him back to his dark activities. Though it was not until the following year, in June 1986, that he managed to capture another victim.

Todd Stoops, a twenty-one-year-old male sex worker, who Berdella had known since 1984, was next in line to die. Stoops was not the typical victim, however. Amazingly, he had already identified Berdella as the perpetrator of the murders he had read about in the newspaper and whom law enforcement was hunting down. Nevertheless, something—most likely Berdella himself—convinced the young man to go to Berdella's home. Berdella felt a great physical attraction toward Todd, and this caused him to make his torture of the youth more 'intimate.'

Todd was the first victim to be held for more than just a few days—the young man suffered humiliating indecencies for two whole weeks before his death.

Berdella's methods had evolved even further. He now had total control of his captive through fear and pain. He didn't need to exclusively incapacitate Todd with sedatives, instead, combining them with the threat of horrible acts, such as administering electrical shocks through Todd's eyes in an attempt to blind him and starving him to the point of not even allowing the captive a glass of water. On one particular occasion, after failing to blind the young man, Berdella injected Drano into Todd's larynx, believing he could damage it and leave the youth mute. It was unsuccessful, but the agony was constant and unrelenting.

As if all of these terrible acts weren't enough, Berdella used Todd as a sexual slave, raping and assaulting him constantly during the two weeks he held the man captive. He even forced his fist and forearm up Todd's rectum, rupturing it. Berdella documented all of this, his Polaroid collection growing larger and his diary filling with more and more notes, all of which meant something to him and his 'studies.'

Todd Stoops grew so weak with fever, blood loss, and sickness that he could barely breathe. Eventually, his body gave in; he died in the first week of July 1986, becoming yet another mound of limbs and remains to be thrown into black bags and dumped in the garbage.

Berdella felt happy with himself after Todd Stoops' ordeal and death. He had come so far and accomplished so much more than what he had expected, but the feeling of invincibility remained. After inflicting so much pain and killing several men, he was still a free man; no consequences of any kind weighed him down. In fact, he could keep going if he wanted to, and nobody would stand in his way. Furthermore, he had discovered how impressive the human body was and how much damage it could sustain before failing. There was so much more to do, so much more pain to inflict.

Berdella was now convinced: he was nowhere near done. His next victim was going to suffer even more than his last, and he was going to enjoy it even more.

Unfortunately, his desires would become a reality not long after. Berdella's urges were worsening, his violence escalating. There were no limits to his capabilities.

VII

No Mercy

THE YEAR 1987 ARRIVED. BERDELLA HADN'T tortured or killed anyone since July of the previous year, and it weighed heavily on him. He led a normal life, but the monster in his mind—that had gradually grown over the years and needed to be fed intermittently—was whispering dark thoughts to him and begging him to find a new victim.

Berdella had experienced the great pleasure of humiliating, hurting, and killing men, and would now find it very difficult to stop willingly. It was too late; he had gone too far, and it was just a matter of how long he could continue before he was detected.

Thus, twenty-year-old Larry Wayne Pearson became Berdella's unfortunate next victim.

Larry met Berdella at his store, where he had been immediately attracted to the nature of his wares. He, too, was a collector of esoteric objects, as well as a practitioner of witchcraft. Robert immediately took a liking to the young man, perhaps seeing a younger version of himself standing there in front of him.

A friendship began to develop, and Berdella allowed the young man to stay at his home. At first, Berdella did not see Pearson as his next victim, simply allowing the youth to perform different chores around the house in lieu of rent. Berdella was content, Larry was comfortable, and everything was okay.

That is, until Larry made a big mistake.

On June 23, Berdella bailed Larry out of jail. He'd gotten in trouble and Berdella was quick to help him out. As the two returned home, Berdella heard Larry make a distasteful joke about robbing gay men in Wichita. This joke, and Larry's tone when making it, offended Berdella and lowered his opinion of this young man who was staying in his home.

Berdella didn't allow his expression to change, but Larry's words had angered him. The monster within him shifted and awakened. It was too late to stop his desires from rising to the surface; Larry was already a dead man walking.

Berdella waited until that evening to make his move. He plied the young man with drinks. Once Larry was drunk, Berdella took action. He injected Pearson with chlorpromazine and dragged him down to the basement, tying the young man's hands above his head and securing the rope to a column. Then he pulled out a syringe. It contained drain cleaner destined for Pearson's larynx, in a new attempt at rendering one of his victims mute.

Once he was done injecting the chemical product into Larry's voice box, Berdella went upstairs to get his electrical transformer, which he would use to shock Pearson in terror and submission.

Terror and submission were the two key themes of Pearson's time in captivity. He attempted to coax Berdella in treating him well and perhaps even letting him go. He tried to cooperate with the torturer, allowing him to take sexual advantage of him and withstanding extensive physical abuse without complaint.

Berdella used constant and repeated electrical shocks on Larry while documenting their effects on his mind and body, even breaking the young man's right hand to ensure he remained under his control.

On the fifth day, Berdella began to appreciate Pearson's collaboration and allowed him to continue his ordeal in the second-floor bedroom. He did not endure lesser pain and suffering by any means, but his fear of returning to the basement kept him submissive long after he had been taken upstairs.

The torture lasted for six whole weeks, with Berdella taking more detailed notes than ever. He recorded every single thing he did to Larry, as well as the effects of said actions. He added to his collection of Polaroids with graphic pictures of Pearson, most showing his face contorted in agony and mouth hanging open as he gasped in pain.

Larry tried hard to cooperate in the hope of saving his life—even avoiding moving a single muscle while sleeping or being tortured in an attempt to keep Berdella from increasing the pain—but it wasn't enough. It became too much for Pearson, who increasingly felt frustrated with his captivity and mistreatment.

He had been holding back, allowing Berdella to humiliate, rape, and brutalize him in many ways, but it didn't seem to be getting him any closer to freedom. Finally, Berdella pushed young

Larry Pearson over the edge. On August 5, 1987, the last time Berdella came to his room and attempted to torture him, Pearson resisted, lashing out and attempting to fight back.

It was useless. He was too well-bound and too weak to accomplish anything. Berdella, in his fury, savagely bludgeoned the young man into unconsciousness, put a bag over his head, and suffocated him to death with a ligature.

It angered him to have to kill Pearson, but he would not accept losing control of his captive, even for an instant. Absolute dominance was an integral part of the house rules he imposed; no man would resist him once captured.

The dead captive was taken downstairs to the dreaded basement, where he was dissected. Berdella, in an act of either rage or triumph, severed the corpse's head from its shoulders and put it aside. Once he was done disposing of the body, Berdella went out back and dug up something he'd kept in his yard for a while: Robert Sheldon's skull. He pushed it aside, replacing it in the hole with Pearson's skull. Then, neatly covering the hole, he returned indoors with Sheldon's skull, cleaning it and removing the teeth. These were kept in envelopes in several locations around the room, while the skull itself was placed inside a closet as a souvenir.

Berdella sat back and reflected on what he'd done. His torturing method had been refined and improved since he'd taken his first captive, Jerry Howell. He'd learned how effective electrical shocks were for keeping a victim submissive and that psychological torture was just as effective as physical and sexual types. There was little that a captive could do when faced with the constant terror of pain and suffering. After all, Berdella never let them know when they were going to die or if they were going to be released at all. Playing with their dwindling hope for survival was key to keeping them reluctant to resist him.

Although Berdella had perfected the art of torture, unfortunately, that didn't mean he was going to stop anytime soon. He was long past caring.

As stated previously, from Berdella's perspective, there was a sense of shifted guilt. According to Berdella's logic, it wasn't just him who was guilty of these crimes; it was also law enforcement's fault for not catching him. He had cut out clippings from a local newspaper detailing the case of the missing Jerry Howell, so he was up-to-speed with the investigations. He found it laughable that, despite the fact that he'd been questioned as a prime suspect not long after Howell and Walter James Ferris's disappearances, and had even been placed under surveillance, the local police still hadn't been able to make the necessary connections linking him to the murders.

When Berdella grew tired of the police questioning and surveillance, he used his lawyer to threaten filing harassment accusations against the police. This made law enforcement take a step back and leave him alone.

Berdella thought he was truly invincible, a ghost who walked unseen in daylight and who didn't have to worry about the consequences of his actions. He wanted to torture and kill until he grew tired of it, and with an endless pool of young homosexual men to choose from—due to his connections and friendship with the said community—he believed he wouldn't ever have to worry about finding new victims.

However, Berdella was wrong. He was not invincible, and he would not go on killing forever. His next victim would be his last.

In fact, his next victim would be the very reason Berdella met his downfall.

VIII

Outsmarted

THE LAST MAN TO ENTER BERDELLA'S TORTURE dungeon of a home was no fool. Twenty-two-year-old Chris Bryson's experience as a male sex worker had armed him with a quick wit and the ability to get out of sticky situations with ease. It was, perhaps, why he managed to avoid becoming another cut-up corpse departing Berdella's address in black bags, and why he actually managed to fool The Butcher of Kansas City in to trusting him and giving him the means to escape.

It all started on the evening of March 29, 1988, at a Greyhound bus station in downtown Kansas City. Berdella was out looking for company, although he had other intentions for his victim-to-be than just a bit of sex. Chris Bryson spotted the lonely man cruising in his vehicle and approached, believing he was hustling the stranger. It was actually the other way around; Berdella had already honed in on the young sex worker and knew full well that he would be taking him home to torture

Chris was pleasantly surprised when Berdella suggested they go to his home, having grown accustomed to servicing his clients in cheap motel rooms and car back seats. He also didn't expect what was to follow.

When they arrived, Berdella sat Chris down in the living room and talked with the youth, trying to get to know him a bit better. The intention of sex was still there, of course, but Berdella was making it interesting.

Eventually, Berdella suggested they go upstairs to the bedroom. He casually mentioned the fact that his three vicious Chow-Chows lived on the lower level of the house, adding that the upstairs floor had a television and more comfortable furniture. Unknowingly, Chris consented and began climbing the steps. As he did, he felt somebody move swiftly to his side.

Berdella was quick and ruthless, smacking Chris in the back of the head with an iron bar before sedating him and dragging him up to his bedroom, where he immediately bound him to the bed. When Chris woke up, he found himself naked and helpless. A smiling Berdella stood over him with his Polaroid. As Chris attempted to find out what was going on, the torture began.

Berdella, as the reader may have noticed, was increasing the brutality of his methods with each new victim, and Chris Bryson was no exception to this rule. He began by fitting a dog collar onto Chris's neck and beat the youth with an iron club, aiming to break bones in his hands and legs. He injected Chris with an animal tranquilizer and ensured his continued health with antibiotics to protect the many wounds he'd inflicted on the young man's flesh. Again, Berdella documented what he'd done to Bryson, taking more pictures than ever, and watching the young sex worker's agony with glee.

The first night of torture ended with a long session of brutal rape, including the insertion of objects into the victim's anal cavity.

The next morning was not merciful to Chris. Berdella entered the room and woke him up by jabbing swabs soaked with alcohol into his eyes. He later added ammonia with the intention of making Chris blind. He continued raping the young man, causing him to scream and call out for help. Berdella, always dominant and controlling, quickly grabbed a syringe and injected Drano into Chris' throat, threatening to make him lose his voice entirely. He told Chris that he had tortured and killed several men already. He also told him that the three dogs he'd mentioned on the night before had eaten the captives after Berdella was done with them. Chris believed the tale—a story not so far from the truth, to be fair.

Electricity continued to be a crucial tool in Berdella's torture repertoire; he constantly shocked the young sex worker with alligator clips clamped on to different parts of his body, including his testicles. In the photographs, Bryson's agony is quite clear: his eyes are wide and his body is full of cuts and open wounds. Berdella warned Chris against escaping, telling him that he needed only to think about himself, Berdella, and the house.

After a few days of captivity, Chris seemed to have gained territory with Berdella, who sat on top of him and began to pull out the Polaroids he had taken of his previous victims. Berdella explained to Chris that he had held others in the same situation, and that—if he gained some of Berdella's trust—there was a chance he could save his life and leave captivity. If not, Berdella continued, he would be murdered and disposed of like his predecessors. "I've gotten this far with other people before and they're dead now," the killer said in a cautionary tone. "Because of mistakes they made."

By the evening of the third day, Chris noticed that Berdella was certainly starting to trust him. He'd agreed to loosen the bindings on his arms and tied them in front of him instead of above his head. Next, Chris asked the killer to leave the television on. Berdella allowed Chris to keep the remote control when he was out of the room and even threw him a cigarette and some matches.

Unlike some of the previous victims, who had pinned their hopes on Berdella being merciful and letting them go, Chris had long abandoned any such expectations. He knew he had to escape, no matter what. It became an obsession, one that would keep him going even when the pain was at its fullest. He watched Berdella closely and kept his eyes and ears open when the man wasn't nearby. The fact that Berdella had given him the remote control meant he could keep the television's volume down and listen to his captor's movements. At one point, he stopped hearing Berdella at all. Robert Berdella—torturer, killer, and captor—had left the house to do some errands.

Fortunately for Chris, the looser arrangement of the ropes that bound him allowed him some leeway to get one of his hands free, a fact that he had confirmed earlier, while Berdella wasn't watching. He listened one last time to make sure that his captor was gone, and then Chris knew:

It was time.

He pulled his hand loose and stretched across the bed, pushing aside the cigarette and grabbing the matches his captor had thrown there. Quickly and anxiously, he lit each one, using them to burn the ropes wrapped around his other limbs so that he could escape. Each second was vital, for if Berdella returned, Chris knew that he would be killed.

Finally, with the ropes still dangling from his body, the young man stood up to look through the window. He worried about it being locked or nailed closed, but Berdella had not expected any of his captives to escape and hadn't taken such precautions. A two-floor fall separated him from the ground, but Bryson had no time to think about it; his life was in danger. He smashed the window with ease and leaped out, breaking a bone in his foot as he landed. The pain made him grit his teeth, but he knew that even worse pain awaited him if he stayed, so he kept going, running to a house across the street.

There was a man standing in the street, reading a meter. He spotted Bryson and heard the young man screaming at him to call the police. The meter reader decided to leave the problem in someone else's hands and alerted the nearest neighbors instead.

They were quick to call the police, although they didn't allow Chris to enter their home due to his state of damage and undress. Luckily for the young victim, the police force was quick to arrive at his location.

Four officers questioned Chris almost immediately. He was forced to lie about his occupation, instead, saying that he had been hitchhiking when Berdella had abducted, raped, and tortured him for four days. He described how he'd been injected with drain cleaner, sodomized, and drugged during the entirety of his captivity. His scars, swollen eyes, and the dog collar gave his words the necessary emphasis to give credence to his story. He then told the police officers how he'd escaped out his captor's window.

The officers were quick to swing into action, with some taking Chris to a nearby hospital while the others stayed at the crime scene. They radioed the Kansas City Police Department to request a formal search warrant.

The killer hadn't been arrested yet, but it was already over for him. Chris had succeeded in doing what the six men before him had sadly been unable to do, despite their best resistance.

He had successfully brought Robert Berdella's terror spree to a climactic ending.

IX

Game Over

CHRIS BRYSON WAS QUESTIONED AT LEAST
twice more—once at the hospital where he received
treatment and again at the Kansas City Police Department. In the
former interview, he was simply asked to identify Berdella from
photographs to verify the culprit's true identity. In the second
interrogation, Bryson was told to recount exactly what had
happened to him during his time in captivity in Berdella's home.

The young man made sure not only to tell the police of the
sexual abuse, humiliation, and physical torture that he'd suffered
but also of the Polaroids he'd been shown, of other men in similar
or worse situations. He recalled that several of the men in the

pictures had appeared to be dead when the images were captured. Chris added that Berdella had threatened him at one point with never letting him leave, allowing him to choose between simply accepting his torture and suffering much worse—and possibly outright death—if he resisted.

Berdella was arrested on charges of sexual assault on the day of Chris's escape. Police were bound by Missouri law to determine within twenty-four hours if they had evidence of these charges or not. They were forced to move quickly to obtain their search warrant after Berdella denied them entry to his home.

As soon as the document was ready, investigators entered the killer's home and headed to the second floor to do an extensive search. Since this level had been the place where Chris had been held, they guessed that any concrete evidence to charge Berdella would be there.

They immediately caught sight of the discarded burnt ropes still attached to the bed and an electrical transformer plugged into the wall, with wires and clips on their ends leading to the bed. There was a metal tray nearby that contained used syringes, small bottles of sedatives, swabs, and eye drops. The iron pipe Berdella had used to beat Bryson was in the room, as well as other objects used for bondage. There were also visible signs of other captives having been held in the bedroom, leading police officers to begin to accept the notion that Chris Bryson had been the last of several victims.

While half of the force sent to Berdella's home checked inside, the others searched outside, especially in his backyard. A grid was created to aid the investigators. During their search, they dug up Pearson's decomposed human head with intact hair and tissue he'd placed there. Moments later, the other officers found Sheldon's older, cleaner skull upstairs on the second floor. They found several human vertebrae marked with knife cuts in a hallway, and they also discovered the envelopes containing teeth from Robert Sheldon's skull.

Police officers didn't have an easy job, considering Berdella's home was filthy with dog feces and cluttered with large amounts of objects of all kinds.

Descending to the basement, the police officers came across more worrying finds: a hacksaw and a miter saw were stored next to a chainsaw, the latter still dirty with blood, flesh, and pubic hair. An officer suggested a luminol test, which found extensive traces of blood, especially in the area Berdella had used to dispose of his victims.

All in all, however, none of that was as important as what they found next. There were over three hundred and fifty Polaroid pictures stowed in various locations around the home, containing images of Bryson and the other men, before and after they'd died. An extremely detailed notepad was found in a bedroom, containing the logs Berdella had kept for each individual victim. This piece of evidence would become crucial in putting him away. Walter James Ferris's wallet and driver's license were also highly-incriminating items.

There was only one unresolved issue: no bodies had been found. It was difficult to convince a judge of a murder charge when there was no body to prove that a murder had occurred at all. There was still work to do.

One of the first steps that the KCPD's task force took to resolve the case was to link Berdella to the victims through his own notes and Polaroids. He was already a known hustler and had a reputation for either preying on or helping young men, depending on who you asked. The records of both previous occasions in which the local police had questioned Berdella and come up with nothing were also revisited, and police were forced to look elsewhere.

Both Walter James Ferris and Jerry Howell were identified by their family members as the men both living and dead in several of Berdella's images. Apart from the men who appeared in the pictures, there were many names written on Berdella's notepads, names that became relevant to the investigation. Police officers tracked each name down to its owner, and eventually, they came across a man named Freddie Kellogg, who had been a close acquaintance of Berdella's. He was questioned and rapidly became the most important witness of all. He claimed that he had been present and had assisted Berdella in drugging young men lodging in his home so that they could engage in consenting or non-consenting intercourse with them.

Kellogg added that Berdella had tasked him with finding attractive males for their parties at the killer's home. He even managed to identify the men in the Polaroids as Todd Stoops, Robert Sheldon, and Larry Wayne Pearson. Investigations would determine that Berdella had indeed secured a bond for Pearson in June 1987 and that he had gone missing after that.

With that evidence, Berdella was truly cornered. Now there was no easy escape from justice. The police informed him of their discoveries soon after the search and charged him with one count of felonious restraint, one count of assault, and seven counts of forcible sodomy. More charges would come later—including a formal charge of murder by dismemberment for Larry Pearson's murder—but for now, this was enough. Robert Berdella had fallen.

With the media crawling all over his home and investigating his life to make his murders public, Berdella knew that the terrible moment he'd been dreading had come.

Despite Berdella's gargantuan effort to hide his true character—by behaving and helping in his community—the world knew that he was, in fact, a monster.

Chris Bryson and the law had unmasked the killer; now the legal system had to make sure he paid for his crimes...

...and pay he would.

X

Falling To Pieces

JACKSON COUNTY JAIL WAS THE PLACE WHERE Robert Berdella would await his fate. For his own safety, Berdella was kept in a private area of the sickbay—otherwise, word of his crimes would inflame the other prisoners into attacking or even killing him. He was visited by several friends and acquaintances, and Berdella seemed remorseful and pensive.

Upon further questioning, it became obvious that Robert was uncomfortable about what the community—who until then had respected him and looked up to him as a civic role model—would think of him now. The fact he had lost complete control of his life and his situation didn't help, either. All in all, it was too humiliating for Berdella, and he couldn't bring himself to talk to anybody.

Berdella had made many friends in Kansas City during his lifetime, many not believing he had committed the crimes the media were talking about. Some even theorized that the police were framing Berdella; after all, his behavior had been so upstanding before the grisly murders took place. Support came from several quarters, but the police were getting closer and closer to revealing the true Berdella. His reputation was about to be destroyed, as it arguably should have already been, long before his arrest.

Eventually, Berdella was called in to help with the investigation. Police officers suggested that Berdella help them identify the people in the pictures he had taken. They asked him to imitate the poses that the person capturing the images had been in when they had been taken, including the obscene, sexually-graphic pictures. This humiliated Berdella even further, making the investigation all the more draining for him.

Perhaps all of this did have some kind of effect on the killer's conscience because the next time he appeared in court for the hearing into the murder of Larry Wayne Pearson, on July 23, 1988, Berdella was quick to plead guilty. Whether it was a strategy or simply just Berdella enjoying his final moment of control, nobody knew. The judge and prosecuting attorneys were left dumbfounded and asked he confess under oath. Without any hesitation, Berdella told the court that he had placed a plastic bag over Pearson's head and suffocated him with a rope.

"Did you perform this act intentionally?" the judge asked Berdella.

"Yes."

It was all that was required. Robert Berdella was sentenced to life imprisonment without the possibility of parole. Upon sentencing, he was transferred to Missouri State Penitentiary, although for his own safety, he would soon be placed in protective custody at Potosi Correctional Center. There were many prisoners who would have happily brutalized Robert or taken his life—arguably, he had done exactly the same to his victims and may have deserved such a fate.

Berdella pled guilty again the next month in a second hearing pertaining to the charges of forced sodomy against Chris Bryson, earning him another life term without parole.

Despite his two initial guilty pleas, Robert pleaded not guilty to the remaining five murder charges in September 1988. This weighed heavily against him; Berdella was looking down the barrel of a death penalty. The defense requested a plea bargain. In exchange for the prosecution agreeing not to seek the death penalty, Berdella was to testify how he had kidnapped, tortured, and murdered each of his victims.

What followed was a gruesome recount of how he had used his 'play toys'—as he called his captives—to satisfy his desires. Three days and over seven hundred pages of transcript were necessary to allow him to tell the entire tale of how he had ruined the lives of seven men and killed six of them in the process. He spoke of how he had been influenced by Stanley Mann's 1965 film, *The Collector*. He said after the initial feelings of disgust from killing young Jerry Howell, he had been able to move on and grow stronger in an attempt to mimic what he had seen in the film.

Much of his journal had been filled with abbreviations and unintelligible descriptions; Berdella helped the court understand exactly what these meant, revealing that he had violated his victims with vegetables, injected them with chemicals, and filled their ears with caulk, among other atrocities.

As the days passed and his confession was completed, the media and others confronted Berdella, wanting to know more about this monster. In Berdella's own eyes, he was still a good man and couldn't explain his homicidal tendencies. He truly lamented the fact that his image had been destroyed and attempted to fix this by setting up a trust fund with fifty thousand dollars for the victims' families. Understandably, they found the sum laughable for the damage he had done. Several media outlets even linked Berdella with Satanism, due to the almost ritualistic nature of his killings, but he quickly discredited these reports.

Ultimately, Robert Berdella served only four years of his life sentence. He had complained many times about the conditions of his captivity, having been attacked on at least one occasion, and denied access to his heart medication. At two p.m. on October 8, 1992, Robert began to complain of chest pains and received medical assistance at the prison infirmary a few minutes later. Medical staff determined his heart was unstable, and he would need to be taken to a hospital. An ambulance from a nearby medical center in Columbia was sent to pick him up, but it was too late.

Robert Berdella, forty-three-years-old, died of heart failure at 3:55 p.m.

Curiously, the judge at his trial—Alvin Randall—was asked what he thought about Berdella's death. His answer was simple and sarcastic: *"Couldn't have happened to a nicer guy."*

Conclusion

DEATH CAME FOR ROBERT BERDELLA, AS IT HAD for all of his victims. The saddest aspect of this case was that their corpses were never found, instead are left rotting in a landfill somewhere in Ohio.

One must wonder if the victims were given some kind of bitter justice when Berdella's heart stopped beating, or if it would have been better if he'd been forced to live out the rest of his life reflecting on what he'd done in the cramped confines of a cell.

To the very end, Robert was remorseless for his actions, only having displayed sadness or regret because his public image had been torn to pieces. He was a true monster, a dark creature hidden in human flesh, who tore apart the lives of his seven victims and their families, unknowingly dehumanizing himself in the process.

Let it be said that the world is better without Robert Berdella and that his victims rest in peace despite their horrific ends.

Hopefully, by learning about men like Berdella, the world can seek to help others who plan to act out similar fantasies, before they turn into monsters like The Kansas City Butcher.

Edmund Kemper

The True Story of The Brutal Co-Ed Butcher

Introduction

THE STORY OF EDMUND KEMPER IS AN illustration of how individuals can slip through the cracks of society, resulting in deadly consequences. The evil that drove Edmund Kemper to claim ten lives was the product of a tragic history. Kemper is just one of two thousand six hundred twenty-five serial killers in the history of the United States, which has more serial killers than any other part of the world.

According to the FBI, a serial killing is "A series of three or more killings, not less than one of which was committed within the United States, having common characteristics, suggesting the reasonable possibility the crimes were committed by the same actor or actors."

Research by the Internal Association of Forensic Science produced a list of fourteen characteristics that increase the likelihood of becoming a serial killer:

1. Over ninety percent of serial killers are male.

2. Serial killers tend to be intelligent, with IQs in the "bright normal" range.

3. Serial killers tend to do poorly in school, have trouble holding down jobs, and often work as unskilled laborers.

4. Serial killers tend to come from markedly unstable families.

5. As children, many serial killers were abandoned by their fathers and raised by domineering mothers.

6. Families of serial killers often have criminal, psychiatric, and alcoholic histories.

7. Serial killers often hate their fathers and mothers.

8. Serial killers are commonly abused as children—psychologically, physically, and sexually—the abuse is oftentimes by a family member.

9. Many serial killers spend time in institutions as children, with records of early psychiatric problems.

10. Serial killers generally have a high rate of suicide attempts.

11. From an early age, many serial killers are intensely interested in voyeurism, fetishism, and sadomasochistic pornography.

12. More than sixty percent of serial killers wet their beds beyond the age of twelve.

13. Many serial killers are fascinated with starting fires.

14. Serial killers are involved in sadistic activity or tormenting small creatures.

Of these fourteen indicators, Edmund Kemper met twelve of them.

The term "serial killer," was originated by FBI profiler Robert Ressler in the 1970s. Until then, such crimes were referred to as mass murders. Ressler, who interviewed Kemper, derived the term "serial killer" from the label "serial adventurer." Used by the movie industry, "serial adventures" described short episodic films that ran as a series—each series building on the one that came before it. An example of serial adventurers is the Batman series. Ressler observed that crimes often follow a similar pattern.

In today's terms, mass murder is used in reference to multiple killings that occur during one incident. An example is James

Holmes, who shot into the audience of a movie theater in Aurora, Colorado, on July 20, 2012.

Profiling serial killers, Ressler believes each murder that the serial killer commits is motivation to kill again. Part of this desire is driven by the goal to commit the perfect murder—as it relates to the killer's fantasy. This desire was part of Kemper's mindset, as each co-ed that he killed was used as a mechanism to hone his skills in killing

The FBI's Behavioral Unit-2 released a multi-perspective study on serial killers and indicted the media for spreading myths through interviews with pseudo-experts, lacking the kind of in-depth research that the FBI conducts. One of those myths is that serial killers are loners who are unable to function in society. Robert Yates, Gary Ridgeway aka the Green River Killer, and Dennis Rader aka the BTK Killer, all lived functional lives within their communities. Edmund Kemper was no different, stating he always felt he lived in a parallel universe. Part of Kemper functioned at school and work, while the other part was lost in dark fantasies.

Another myth is that serial killers are unable to stop killing. In contrast, the FBI points out that certain factors in the lives of serial killers can cause them to halt the killing; when they are caught. The

BTK killer, Dennis Rader, killed ten people over a seventeen-year period, between 1974 and 1991. He was caught in 2005, at which time he was married. Another serial killer, Jeffrey Gorton, killed his last victim in 1991 but was not captured until 2002.

Research on serial killers is leading the way in understanding why serial killers can commit multiple murders before being caught. The first finding is that serial killers are highly skilled in presenting themselves as being normal individuals, preventing them from being viewed with suspicion. The second finding is that there are usually no connections between the serial killer and his victims.

In a study of one hundred seven serial killers, ninety percent of their victims were unknown to them. Furthermore, long-term studies on serial killers indicate that the victims of serial killers tend to be equal gender-wise; female victims slightly outnumbering male victims. As for victim ethnicity, most victims are white, with a quarter being black. In regards to victim age, serial killers tend to target young victims. The number of victims over the age of thirty drops dramatically.

FBI research also indicates there is no general profile for a serial killer: each serial killer is driven by their own motivation, and serial killers are not limited to a specific demographic group.

Additionally, some serial killers, like Kemper, are unable to separate violence from sexual gratification. Killing women was the only way Kemper felt safe to connect with co-eds.

Suffering from a severe fear of being rejected, Kemper did not know how to communicate with his victims. For Kemper, who had never kissed a girl or been on a date, killing women was the only way he could relate to them.

So, what causes a person to become a serial killer? Research indicates there is no simple answer to this question because it involves several factors. However, there is one key point that researchers agree upon: if we want to stop creating serial killers, we need to learn to live peacefully in society, especially in the home. Ending domestic violence is the surest way to end serial killing.

Experts in criminology, social, and behavioral psychology, agree that ongoing psychological trauma during childhood is a hallmark of serial killers. To gain relief from this trauma, these children often commit violence against pets or other animals.

Another serial killer, Jeffry Dahmer, as a child, would leave home when his parents fought and take refuge in the woods, where he found comfort with the pelts of animals he had killed.

Likewise, Kemper killed two family cats.

I

The Home Where Demons Were Sown

"WHAT DO YOU THINK HIS SENTENCE should be?" A reporter asked the judge. The judge replied that, if he had it his way, Kemper would be tortured to death.

Instead of fulfilling his wish, during the penalty phase of the trial, the judge sentenced Edmund Kemper to eight concurrent life sentences. Kemper's sentencing took place in November of 1973. The judge was not able to sentence Kemper to the death penalty because California had already eliminated capital punishment.

At the time of his sentencing, Edmund Kemper was twenty-five years old. He was found guilty on eight counts of first-degree murder and would become known as the "Co-ed Killer," though his victims were not restricted to college co-eds.

For Edmund Kemper, the descent into madness occurred early on.

Born December 18, 1948, in Burbank, California, Edmund Kemper was large from the start, weighing in at thirteen pounds. By the time he was four, Edmund was a head taller than his peers. Edmund was the middle child of Edmund Emil Kemper II and Clarnell Kemper; he had two sisters. His father, E.E. Kemper II, was a veteran of World War II. After the war, the Kempers settled in Burbank, which at the time was a small town located in Los Angeles County. E.E. worked at the Pacific Proving Grounds, where he tested nuclear weapons. He later became an electrician. The town of Burbank had grown during the war; Lockheed Aircraft had chosen it as a site for the production of planes. By 1943, Burbank had a population of 53,899.

Both of Edmund's parents were strict disciplinarians, and their marriage was strained. Clarnell Kemper was known to be a difficult woman. It has been suggested that Clarnell may have suffered from borderline personality disorder. Edmund's father would later state that testing bombs were nothing compared to being married to

Clarnell. He even said that being married to Clarnell had more of an impact on him "than three hundred and ninety-six days and nights of fighting on the front did."

Edmund felt close to his father, as his mother was distant towards him, rarely showing him any affection. Consequently, Kemper's feelings for his mother fueled a rage that would escalate with the passing of time—a rage foretelling the destiny of both him and his mother.

If Edmund's rage was a ticking time bomb, then the lighting of the fuse was the divorce of his parents in 1957. Edmund was only nine when his father moved out; his mother was left with full custody. Clarnell moved Edmund and his two sisters to Montana. It was during this time that Edmund started to express his anger and violent tendencies.

At age ten, Edmund buried the family's pet cat alive; he later dug up the dead cat and played with it. When he was thirteen, he killed another family cat because it favored the company of his sister, Allyn. Edmund butchered the cat with a machete knife and placed its remains in a closet.

When his mother made the grisly discovery, Edmund denied any responsibility for the cat's death. Years later, as an adult,

Edmund would reveal in an interview that he took pride in the fact that he could successfully lie about the cat's death, and that he could appear to be an average person despite the rage and fear he felt inside.

As a child, Edmund considered himself a chronic daydreamer, often fantasizing about committing acts of violence against others, in particular, his mother. He would set fires and engage in play that was violent, like dismembering his sisters' dolls, or pretending he was in a gas chamber and mimicking the convulsive movements of a dying prisoner.

At ten, Edmund's mother made him sleep in the basement of their home out of fear he might harm his sisters. To prepare the basement for him, Edmund's mother placed a mattress in the dark, barren room. Edmund would later recall the single, bare bulb that provided light in the rat-infested quarters was his bedroom.

A few years later, when Edmund was fourteen, he could no longer tolerate living with his mother. He decided to run away so he could be with his father, thinking this would make his life easier. His hopes for a better life were short-lived—dashed when he arrived at his father's home in California to discover Edmund II had remarried and had a stepson through his new wife.

Edmund's father was less than enthusiastic to see his son but allowed Edmund to stay with him for a while before eventually sending him back to his mother in Montana.

Upon returning to his mother's home, Edmund discovered that his mother was also planning to remarry. Like her ex-husband, Edmund II, Clarnell was not interested in having Edmund back. To remedy the situation, Clarnell decided to wash her hands of Edmund and sent him to live with his paternal grandparents in North Fork, California.

Barely a teenager, Edmund was unwelcomed by his parents. His father, the only person whom he felt close to, was starting a new life without him. His mother, who he held such deep anger for, was about to marry her third husband. Edmund was unwanted, friendless, and doing poorly in school. He wanted a connection with other people, especially girls or women, but felt completely inadequate. His mother's cruel and domineering ways had burned a hole in Kemper's soul.

He went deeper into his fantasies of violence and killing. What he could not anticipate was that his fantasies would materialize into reality upon arriving at his grandparents' ranch.

II

The Carnage Begins

THE TOWN OF NORTH FORK IS LOCATED IN central California at the foothills of the Sierra Nevada. The town had three restaurants, two gas stations, and one grocery store. The home that Edmund's grandparents, Edmund Kemper Sr. and his wife Maude, offered the fourteen-year-old Edmund was not dramatically different from that of his mother's. Maude was also an authoritarian in her discipline and emasculated him just like his mother had.

Edmund spent as much time as possible outside to avoid dealing with his grandparents, particularly Maude. His grandfather had bought him a .22-gauge rifle so he could go hunting; however, his grandfather had taken the gun away from Edmund when he discovered he had been shooting birds and animals that were not game animals. Edmund's shooting had been just for the sake of killing, especially birds. Later, Edmund's grandfather allowed him to have his rifle back, thinking that Edmund had learned his lesson.

On the morning of August 27, 1964, Maude was in the kitchen, working on a children's book she was writing while her husband had gone grocery shopping. Edmund entered the kitchen and opened the refrigerator, looking for something to eat. Maude made a comment about his sleeping in late and being useless when it came to helping out around the house. Edmund felt his mind drifting to the dark space, filled with the hate for his mother. He felt a surge of rage and stormed back to his room, leaving his grandmother thinking she could get under his skin.

Minutes later, Edmund returned to the kitchen with his .22-caliber rifle. Maude thought nothing of it, figuring he was going hunting. "Don't shoot any birds!" she said to him firmly. Edmund pointed his rifle at Maude and pulled the trigger. The first bullet went through her head. Still pumped with emotion, he fired two more shots into her back. Edmund felt like he was in a daze when he realized what he had just done. He dragged her body to her bedroom and placed her in the closet. Something about killing his grandmother left him with a sense of satisfaction.

Then his thoughts turned to his grandfather, who would be returning at any time. Out of a distorted sense of compassion, Edmund felt he must also kill his grandfather. He did not want him to go through the experience of finding his wife murdered. Edmund looked out the living room window and saw his grandfather's car pulling in. Edmund stepped out the front door, pointed the rifle at his grandfather as he got out of the car. After the shot rang out, his grandfather collapsed to the pavement.

At the age of fifteen, Edmund Kemper had taken the lives of two people.

With both grandparents dead now, the reality of what he had done hit Edmund; he did not know what to do. He called his mother and told her what he had just done. His mother told him to call the police, which he did. Edmund sat in the kitchen as he waited for them to arrive.

He was arrested and taken to the police station, where he was interrogated. When asked why he had killed his grandmother, Edmund replied, "I just wanted to see what it felt like to kill her."

III

When Institutions Fail

EDMUND WAS PLACED IN JUVENILE HALL pending the California Youth Authority's determination of where to place him long-term. Psychiatrists at the California Youth Authority diagnosed Edmund as being paranoid schizophrenic, with an IQ of 136—near genius level.

They decided to place him at Atascadero State Hospital. Fifteen-year-old Edmund entered Atascadero State Hospital on December 6, 1964.

Atascadero State Hospital is a maximum-security facility located on the central coast of California that houses mentally ill convicts. In the late 1990s, there was an exodus of clinical staff from the hospital because they felt that housing sexually violent predators went against the hospital's mission of providing the highest quality care to those who had serious mental illness, and it diverted time and resources.

Experts who are familiar with Edmund's case believe that his referral to Atascadero State Hospital was an irresponsible decision. At the time Edmund was admitted to Atascadero, there were sixteen hundred patients. Of those patients, twenty-four were murderers, and eight hundred were sex offenders. The hospital only had ten psychiatric staff members to serve this population.

Not only did Edmund lack the quality of treatment needed for an offender of his age, but his short stay at Atascadero only strengthened his ability to carry out his future crimes. Edmund spent four years at Atascadero. During that time, he gained the trust of his counselor, even befriending him. His ability to act as a model patient earned him the position as assistant to the staff, which meant he had access to psychological test papers and diagnosis criteria.

Since Edmund was very bright, he was able to educate himself on how to fool the clinicians into believing he was fully rehabilitated. He passed all their psychological testing with flying colors, leading the hospital's medical team to believe that there was no longer a need to contain him.

Despite the recommendation provided by his doctor at Atascadero, the California Youth Authority released Edmund to the custody of his mother in 1969. His doctor had urged them not to release Edmund to his mother, given her past abusive behavior and psychological issues.

There had been no psychiatrist on the panel for Edmund's parole hearing, and no aftercare plan offered. Edmund was twenty-one, had killed two people, spent four years in a maximum-security hospital, and was being returned to the person he hated the most, his mother.

Clarnell had moved from Montana to Santa Cruz, California. Her marriage to her third husband had not worked out and ended in divorce. Clarnell found a job as an administrator at the University of California. Edmund was once again subjected to emotional abuse from Clarnell. She frequently attacked his sense of self-worth, just like she had with her three ex-husbands.

Edmund attended a community college and worked a series of odd jobs as part of his parole requirements. With his juvenile criminal record expunged, Edmund eventually landed a job with the California Department of Transportation in 1971.

Edmund wanted to be a state trooper. He had applied but was disqualified due to his weight. At six feet nine inches tall, and three hundred pounds, his weight was way above the standard; recruits needed to be between two hundred eleven and two hundred thirty-four pounds.

By now, Edmund wanted to get his own place. Through his job at the California Department of Transportation, he was able to save enough money to move into an apartment in the city of Alameda, located near San Francisco. He shared the apartment with a roommate. However, he was unable to pay his rent consistently, and Edmund had to move back in with his mother.

Edmund found himself facing a life he felt was as confining as being in Atascadero. He had failed in his ability to support himself. He wanted to socialize and meet girls, but he lacked any confidence with women. He had never kissed a girl or even been on a date.

As a twenty-one-year-old, having spent the last four years in a mental hospital, and living with his mother, how could he ever hope to start a relationship, especially with his background? At least in

Atascadero, his basic needs were met, without the criticism from a belittling mother.

IV

Days of Training

EDMUND'S ANGER TOWARD HIS MOTHER ONLY grew more intense. She had made him feel like a failure throughout his life. The anger he held for her carried over to women in general, although he did want to socialize and have a relationship with them. As an outlet for his frustration, he engaged in voyeurism, and Santa Cruz was the perfect place for this.

As a magnet for young people, Santa Cruz is located on the northern edge of Monterey Bay and south of San Jose. Santa Cruz offered a great environment for those who enjoy an outdoor lifestyle and are open to free-thinking. The climate is moderate, and there are majestic coastlines, towering redwood forests, and plenty of wide, open spaces.

Hippies, flower children, and college students were attracted to Santa Cruz for its alternative community lifestyles and socially liberal attitudes, as well as its university. In 1970, the population of Santa Cruz was just over thirty-two thousand, a small university town nestled amid California's natural beauty, where young people felt safe there and hitchhiking was common.

While working for the California Department of Transportation, Edmund bought a motorcycle. One day while out riding, Edmund was involved in an accident when a car hit him. Edmund received a fifteen-thousand-dollar settlement from a civil suit he filed against the driver. He used the money to purchase a Ford Galaxy.

Edmund's violent fantasies became stronger and more frequent. In the beginning, he cruised the highways and roads for young females who were hitchhiking, with no other intention than looking at them, engaging in voyeurism. At some point, conflicting forces took over, and the rage and anger he felt for this mother trumped his desires to merely look at the young women.

Edmund purchased a gun and a knife and was able to obtain a pair of handcuffs. He became obsessed with putting his dark fantasies into action.

Edmund did not start out killing the girls he picked up. He would later tell authorities he had picked up around one hundred and fifty hitchhikers, letting each one of them go without incident.

He picked up female hitchhikers he found attractive; he gravitated to small, petite girls. As he drove them to their destination, he observed their behavior and how they reacted to him. He learned ways to make them trust him and to gain their confidence. While he was trying to make his passengers feel comfortable, his violent fantasies of what he really wanted to do to them became more intense.

With each hitchhiker Edmund picked up, he was rehearsing how he would kill them. He gained insight by reading police novels, finding tips such as keeping his car door locked once he had a passenger inside, or how to give others the impression he was safe. He rehearsed killings hundreds of times before actually doing it.

For over a year, Edmund practiced the art of picking up girls. During each of these times, the girl reached her destination safely. That is, until May 7, 1972, the day the killings started.

Edmund was working through a mental tug-of-war. He would later say in an interview with detectives, "I was scared to death of having a relationship with a woman. I am picking up young women, and going a little farther each time. It's a daring kind of thing. First, there wasn't a gun. We go to a vulnerable place, where there aren't people watching, where I could act out and then say, 'No, I can't do this.' Then a gun is in the car, hidden, and this craving; this awful raging, eating feeling is in me, and this fantastic passion takes over. It was overwhelming. It was like a drug. Addicting."

V

From Fantasy to Reality

WHEN MARY ANN PESCE AND HER FRIEND Anita Luchese failed to arrive in Berkley, California, their parents filed missing person reports.

Both girls were students at Fresno State College and hitchhiking to Stanford University. They had planned to spend a few days in Berkley. Police did not give the missing girls report a high priority because of the high number of runaways and the transience nature of the Bay Area. Additionally, the police thought it was not uncommon for teenage girls to spend time with either friends or boyfriends, without telling anyone. While the lack of a rapid response by the police must have been deeply frustrating for the girls' parents, an immediate response would not have made a difference this time.

Edmund had picked up Mary Ann and Anita from the highway on May 7, 1972, and driven them to a secluded area. He tied up Anita and left her in the car. He took Mary Ann, at gunpoint, into the woods. He stabbed her multiple times and left her for dead. He then went back to the car for Anita. He could not believe he had killed Mary Ann. Furthermore, he was fearful that Anita would report him. He was concerned with Anita seeing the blood on his hands. He told Anita he had ended up fighting with Mary Ann and had punched her in the nose. He asked her to go with him to take care of her. However, before Anita could even react, he started stabbing her repeatedly with his knife.

He would tell investigators the knife he used was inadequate for the job. He'd had to stab Anita numerous times to kill her because the knife would not penetrate the overalls she was wearing.

Edmund put the bodies of both girls in the trunk of his car and slammed it shut. He was about to drive away from the scene, but was unable to find his car keys. He panicked, thinking he had left them in the trunk of the car. After several futile attempts to open the trunk, Edmund panicked and ran away. While running, he tripped and fell. In his excitement, he had forgotten about the gun he was carrying and it dropped to the ground. Edmund realized he needed to calm down and gather his wits.

As he settled down, he realized his car keys had been in his back pocket the whole time. He returned to the vehicle. As he drove around with the girls' bodies in the trunk, he tried to figure out what to do next.

Eventually, Edmund decided it was time to bring the bodies to his apartment. Among the items he'd kept in the car, in preparation for committing murder, were blankets. Edmund wrapped the bodies in blankets and carried them one by one into his apartment. Once in his apartment, Edmund removed the girls' clothes, dissected, and decapitated them. He then dumped the bodies in a remote ravine, but kept the heads in his apartment for a few days, before disposing of them. A feeling of power washed over him. He had appeased his inner demons. For now.

Four months had passed since Edmund had killed Mary Ann and Anita. Mary Ann's body and head were discovered; Anita's remains were not found. No one suspected that Edmund was the killer. During Edmund's reign of terror, other serial killers were also committing murders in the areas around Santa Cruz, which may have added to the confusion.

On the evening of September 14, 1972, fifteen-year-old Aiko Koo was hitchhiking along a highway. Aiko was trying to get to her dance class after giving up waiting for the bus. Edmund spotted her on the side of the road. Aiko hesitated before accepting a ride from him.

Edmund's confidence was increasing and he was bolder this time, going directly for his gun. Aiko started to panic, which posed a problem for Edmund. Unable to control his vehicle and Aiko at the same time, Edmund persuaded her he had the gun because he was going to commit suicide. He told her she would not be harmed if she did not attempt to signal for help from nearby cars.

Edmund turned off on to a mountain road and drove until he found a secluded spot. He grabbed and restrained Aiko, wrapping tape around her mouth so she could not speak. Then, he jammed his fingers up her nostrils so she could not breathe; Aiko's struggling ceased when she lost consciousness. But to Edmund's surprise, Aiko regained consciousness just a few minutes later. So, he grabbed her scarf and strangled her, not letting up until he was sure she was dead.

Edmund threw her body in his trunk and drove away. His confidence, not only in his ability to kill, but to get away with it, was growing—so much so that he stopped off for a beer at the Jury Room, a local bar.

The Jury Room bar was a frequent hangout for police offers. Edmund had always been interested in the police and enjoyed talking to them. Murdering Mary Ann and Anita had given him an added incentive to go to the Jury Room; to see if he could catch any conversations about their murders.

The police at the bar referred to him as "Big Ed," and thought of him as a polite, articulate, and gentle individual. After a few drinks, Edmund drove to his mother's home to visit. Neither the police at the Jury Room nor his mother had any idea the car parked outside contained Aiko's body. Edmund even took time to excuse himself from these social visits to take another look at the body.

Like many serial killers, Edmund would often keep trophies of his victims. Besides body parts, he would keep articles of clothing, photographs, and other personal items.

After leaving his mother's home, Edmund drove back to his apartment. He transferred Aiko's body from the trunk of his car to his bed, where he laid her out. As with Mary Ann and Anita, he dissected her body and removed her hands and head, which he disposed of in various locations. Later on, he disposed of the rest of her body. Authorities did not connect Aiko's disappearance to Mary Ann and Anita, and her remains were never found.

The day after killing Aiko, Edmund attended a meeting with psychiatrists—a requirement of his parole. The purpose of the meeting was to appraise Edmund's progress and evaluate if he was adhering to the conditions of his parole. Edmund told the two psychiatrists exactly what they wanted to hear. Not only were they satisfied with his attending college and doing well, but they also liked that he was actively searching for a job and obeying the conditions of his parole.

Both psychiatrists reported that Edmund was not a danger to others and seemed normal. Given that Edmund had killed three women, one as recently as the day before this assessment, the conclusion is all the more staggering.

The following day, the San Madera Police Department received a dealer's "record of sale" for a .44-caliber revolver that was purchased by Edmund Kemper. Sergeant Aluffi was chosen to follow up on Kemper to determine if he was authorized to possess it. Sergeant Aluffi went to Edmund's home, which was difficult to locate, given the layout of the houses in the area. Eventually, he found it. No one was home. Then, he remembered hearing other officers mention that Edmund frequented the Jury Room, so that was his next stop.

Upon his arrival, he saw a vehicle pull into the parking lot. A huge man exited the vehicle; Sergeant Aluffi knew instantly, by the man's size, it was Edmund Kemper. He approached Edmund, who was moving toward the trunk of his car.

Sergeant Aluffi advised Edmund that he needed to take his gun, in order to determine if he was authorized to own it. Edmund replied that the gun was in the trunk of the car. When Edmund moved closer to the trunk, Aluffi advised him to stop moving—that he would open the trunk. He did so, and found the gun wrapped up in a blanket.

When the gun, along with Edmund's background, were checked, no red flags appeared. Since Edmund had been a juvenile when he had killed his grandparents, the record of his crimes had been expunged.

Edmund's next murder would take him back to his mother's home. Growing cocky in his ability to kill undetected, on January 8, 1973, Edmund picked up Cindy Schall, another hitchhiker.

Edmund shot her and took her body to his mother's home; she was out. Edmund carried Cindy's body to his room. Just as with his previous victims, Edmund dissected, dismembered, then decapitated her. The following day, Edmund dumped her bloody body parts in the pristine oceans around Santa Cruz. As for Cindy's head, he buried it in his mother's backyard—directly in front of his bedroom window.

The police would later get a call from beachgoers who came across Cindy's body parts; they'd washed ashore. The police had yet to connect Edmund to any murders, let alone link the victims to each other.

Edmund felt so sure of himself that he continued to visit the Jury Room on a regular basis. In the meantime, the University of Santa Cruz, in partnership with the Santa Cruz police, started an awareness campaign to warn students of the dangers of hitchhiking.

They released this message:

"When possible, girls especially, stay in dorms after midnight with doors locked. If you must be out at night, walk in pairs. If you see a campus police patrol car and wave, they will give you a ride. Use the bus, even if somewhat inconvenient. Your safety is of upmost

importance. If you are leaving campus, advise someone
where you are going, where you can be reached, and the
approximate time of your return. DON'T HITCH A
RIDE, PLEASE!!!"

On February 5th, Edmund got into a heated argument with his mother. Storming out of her house, he hopped in his car. Edmund's urge to kill kicked in; killing provided a release from the intense anger he had for his mother.

During this particular drive, Edmund's windshield was adorned with a parking permit from the University of Santa Cruz, which he had acquired from his mother. It allowed him to drive on campus, looking for potential victims. He cruised around the interior of the campus area and spotted Rosalind Thorpe.

Edmund offered Rosalind a ride. She got in his car, without any hesitation. He drove a little further and spotted Alice Liu— another co-ed hitchhiking. Seeing Rosalind in the passenger seat and the University's parking permit on Edmund's car, Alice got in the backseat without concern.

Edmund was so confident in his ability to kill that he did not even attempt to find a secluded area to park. As they drove along the empty highway, Edmund distracted Rosalind by pointing to a scenic view of the ocean. As Rosalind stared through the passenger window, Edmund shot her in the head, killing her instantly. Alice screamed and tried to escape. He stopped the car and shot her in the head. Alice was still alive, and he shot her three more times in the head. Then Edmund continued driving, as though nothing had happened.

Finding a quiet place on the side of the road, Edmund placed both bodies in the trunk of his car, taking time to wrap them in blankets. He brought the bodies to his mother's home. She was not home, so he carried the bodies to his room where he beheaded them. He had sex with Alice's headless body and then dismembered the two bodies. He also took the time to remove the bullets from both heads. He disposed of the body parts in the area of Santa Cruz, and the heads and hands in the city of Pacifica.

In March, hikers in San Mateo County came across a skull and jawbone near Highway 1; the bones belonged to different people. When detectives searched the area further, they recovered a second skull that belonged to the jawbone found by the hikers. These remains belonged to Rosalind and Alice.

After his arrest, Edmund would tell investigators each of the co-eds he'd killed was a "practice run." He was using them to sharpen his skills. All of this "training" was strengthening him so he would be able to murder the one person who stood at the center of his rage, his mother.

Edmund told the investigators, "I lived as an ordinary person most of my life, even though I was living a parallel and increasingly violent other life." That "increasingly violent other life" would boil over on April 21, 1973.

VI

Mother, This One Is for You

IT WAS NIGHTTIME, AND CLARNELL WAS ABOUT TO retire for the day when Edmund came in. Clarnell made a comment to him, triggering his anger and igniting an argument. Clarnell was tired of Edmund using her home like a hotel and not taking responsibility for himself. Disgusted, she went to her bedroom, closed the door, and got in bed.

Tonight's argument did not have the same impact on Edmund as it had in the past, as he no longer felt like a victim. His killing of six people without bringing any suspicion upon himself made him feel more powerful and more in control than any other time in his life.

Edmund went back to his car and got his tools: a hammer and a knife. He brought them to his room. He turned on the television and watched some shows until it was late and he was confident his mother was asleep. He silently entered her bedroom and stood over her as she lay sleeping. He raised the hammer and brought it down as hard as he could on her head. His mother screamed, writhing in pain and bleeding profusely from her head. Within seconds, she lay motionless. Edmund then took his knife and decapitated her. Holding up her decapitated head, he dug into the opening of her severed neck and pulled out her larynx.

Feeling as though he were in a hyper-aware state, Edmund felt like he was observing himself from afar as he headed for the kitchen. Standing over the kitchen sink, he shoved the larynx down the garbage disposal and turned it on. As small pieces of ground flesh flew out the opening of the garbage disposal, Edmund laughed sadistically. He would tell investigators, "That seemed appropriate as much as she'd bitched, screamed, and yelled at me over so many years."

Edmund then took the head to his room and placed it on top of his dresser. He went to the dartboard that was hanging on the wall and gathered up all the darts. One by one, he threw the darts at his mother's head. In a final explosion of rage, he went back to her bedroom and had sex with her headless corpse. When he had finished using her corpse, Edmund dismembered it and hid the parts in a closet.

Edmund happened to think of Sally Hallett, a close friend of his mother's. Concerned that the fifty-nine-year-old woman would become suspicious when her attempts to reach his mother proved unsuccessful, Edmund called Sally and invited her over for dinner, which she eagerly accepted. When Sally arrived, Edmund strangled her and placed her body in another closet. He then returned to his room, collapsing on his bed; he felt emotionally drained. A lifetime of anger and rage had been released from him like the air from a balloon.

The next morning, Edmund woke up early and took off, leaving the bodies behind. Before he left, he wrote a message and placed it on his mother's bloody mattress. It read, "Sorry champs for the mess. I had to go and did not have time."

Edmund took Sally's car and drove toward Pueblo, Colorado, some fifteen hundred miles away. While driving, he listened to the radio, anticipating there would be a news flash about the murders. He was disappointed by the lack of news coverage about his mother and Sally. However, at the same time, he was beginning to sense the police would catch up with him, given Sergeant Aluffi's inquiry about his gun.

VII

Calling It Quits

UPON REACHING PUEBLO, EDMUND PULLED over to a payphone and called the Santa Cruz Police Department, confessing to the killings of his mother and her friend. The officer who took Edmund's call did not take him seriously, figuring the caller was playing a prank.

Edmund called back again, but the officer who answered continued to express disbelief. The officer knew of Edmund's reputation for hanging around the police at the Jury Room; officers knew Edmund as a jokester, who also gave the impression of being gentle. In addition, the police were unaware of the deaths of Clarnell Strandberg, her name from her third marriage, and Sally

Hallett. Edmund requested that Sergeant Aluffi go to his mother's home—telling him this was no joke.

As Edmund requested, Sergeant Aluffi and another officer went to the home of Clarnell Strandberg. When they entered the home, they were hit with a putrid smell. Instantly, Sergeant Aluffi realized that Edmund's claims were true. When they entered the bedroom, they saw dried blood splattered everywhere. They found the note that Edmund had written: "Sorry champs for the mess. I had to go and did not have time."

When they entered Edmund's room, they began to feel physically nauseated. There, perched on the dresser, was the decaying head of Clarnell Strandberg, covered with darts. They left Edmund's bedroom and made their way down the hall to the two closets. The first closet contained the body of Sally Hallett, and the second had the headless corpse of Clarnell Strandberg.

Sergeant Aluffi called for the coroner and forensic team to start processing the crime scene. The officer who had taken Edmund's original call was notified and instructed that should Edmund call again, they were to keep him on the phone and get any information they could. In the meantime, Sergeant Aluffi contacted the Pueblo Police to inform them about Edmund.

Edmund did call again. The officer who took his call got Edmund's location, which he freely offered. Edmund understood that the Pueblo Police would be notified. He offered to wait for them to arrive at the motel where he was staying. When police descended on the hotel, they found Edmund, calmly waiting for them. He was arrested without incident.

District Attorney Peter Chang and a group of detectives traveled to Pueblo to pick up Edmund and transport him back to Santa Cruz. Edmund continued to be cooperative and waived his right to an attorney.

He is the only serial killer to have ever turned himself in.

VIII

Tying Up Loose Ends

WHEN THEY ARRIVED BACK IN SANTA CRUZ, detectives interviewed Edmund, who spoke freely to them. He confessed to killing the female hitchhikers and took detectives to the sites where he had disposed of their body parts. He told them of the rush he'd experienced when having oral sex with their decapitated heads, feeling like he possessed them as his property.

Edmund also disclosed to detectives the urge to kill women after he experienced clashes with his mother. Edmund freely answered all the detectives' questions; he was an open book without a hint of remorse. During police interviews, Edmund explained he did not know how to connect with women, nor did he know how to communicate with them. He was scared of being rejected.

Edmund's conflicting desire to connect with women, while being afraid of them, would later be expressed during an interview, with the magazine *Cosmopolitan*. The reporter asked him how he felt after killing his mother, when he saw an attractive girl. His answer to the reporter was, "One side of me says, 'I'd like to talk to her, date her.' The other side says, 'I wonder how her head would look on a stick.'"

As detectives dug deeper through their interview, Edmund shared that he felt the fear of rejection he'd experienced was caused by his mother's behavior toward him. Since he had been a child, he had never been able to stand up for himself. He loathed who he was. He always ran away when other kids tried to fight him. Fearing that he was gay, Edmund's mother tried to "make him a man" by being tough on him. He explained how, at eight years old, his mother had ordered him to kill his pet chicken, which she later made him eat. After this ordeal, he ran out of the house, hopped on his bicycle, and rode away with tears streaming down his face.

Edmund also expressed he had never kissed a girl, never gone on a date, nor had he ever had sex. As much as he wanted to socialize and connect with girls, he felt useless and undesirable. For him, violence was the only way he could associate with women. As much as he wanted to relate with the hitchhikers who entered his car, he felt they were all untouchable. The depth of his desire to be with these co-eds was only matched by the anger and rage that he would never be able to make that happen.

The only way he could ever be with these girls would be if he was in total control—which required killing them. Having sex was with a corpse meant no chance of rejection. In fact, as much as he wanted to rape the girls, he feared he would not be able to perform.

In killing his mother, Edmund felt like he was finally in charge; exorcising his demons and standing up to her. This was his way of expressing to her who he was; no longer a scared, abused boy. He was powerful!

When asked why he had turned himself in, Edmund stated, "The original purpose was gone... It wasn't serving any physical, or real, or emotional purpose. It was just a pure waste of time... Emotionally, I couldn't handle it much longer. Toward the end there, I started feeling the folly of the whole damn thing, and at the point of near exhaustion, near collapse, I just said to hell with it and called it all off."

Edmund's original purpose was to get back at his mother, which he achieved. The fact he had frequented the Jury Room, socializing with the officers there, prevented him from falling under their suspicion for any of the killings.

Throughout the interview, Edmund told detectives he was living in parallel realities. When he was killing women or holding their decapitated heads, he felt like he was in another world, totally devoid of reality. Yet, he could snap back to reality instantly. He recalled a time when he was enjoying playing with the head of one of his victims and heard a knock at the door. He answered. It was his apartment manager, who Edmund was able to talk with calmly about her concerns, without arousing any suspicion. When she left, he went back to playing with the head.

Another time, Edmund was walking upstairs to his apartment and carrying a camera bag that belonged to one of his victims; inside the bag was his victim's head. As he approached his apartment, he passed a young couple who were going out on a date. The couple smiled at him, and he responded back with a friendly smile of his own. Deep inside, he longed to be on a date like they were. His ability to seem invisible to others, despite the horrors that he was committing, boosted Edmund's confidence in his ability to kill and get away with it.

He told police it had reached a point of flaunting his killings. He recalled burying the heads of two of his victims in the front yard of his mother's home while she was there. Furthermore, her neighbors' living room window faced him, with the curtains drawn open. The neighbors had been home as well.

Edmund told detectives his urge to kill always followed an argument with his mother. In fact, the co-eds he killed had somehow represented what his mother coveted. Most of his victims were students of the University of Santa Cruz, where his mother worked. His mother would not introduce him to any of the girls she knew there because she felt he was not good enough for them. Edmund stated he wanted to love his mother, but was unable to; calling her an angry, sick woman, and that he hated her. He saw how she was destroying herself with alcohol. However, he also acknowledged that she'd had a difficult life.

IX

A Killer on Trial

ON MAY 7, 1973, EDMUND WAS INDICTED ON eight counts of first-degree murder. Attorney Jim Jackson was the Chief Public Defender for Santa Cruz County. Jackson offered a plea of insanity. Jackson was limited to the insanity defense because Edmund had waived his rights to an attorney when he had been arrested and had spoken freely to the police. Offering an insanity defense would be a hard sell because Edmund had carried out the murders in a strategic and carefully planned manner.

States like California apply the M'Naghten rule, which includes:

"A criminal defendant is not guilty by reason of insanity,

if at the time of the alleged criminal act, the defendant was

so deranged that he or she did not know the nature or

quality of his or her actions, or, if he or she knew the nature

and quality of his or her actions, he or she was so deranged

that he or she did not know that what he or she was doing

was wrong."

Jackson also challenged the diagnosis that had been given to Edmund at Atascadero, successfully arguing that Edmund's violent fantasies were not sufficient to diagnose him as being psychotic.

Edmund attempted to take his life twice while waiting for his trial. He tried to slit his wrists; however, both attempts were unsuccessful. His trial began on October 23, 1973.

The prosecution had three psychiatrists examine Edmund before the trial, and they concurred in their assessments that Edmund was sane. One of the psychiatrists, Dr. Joel Fort, stated that Edmund had most likely engaged in cannibalism by eating parts of his victim and that he had experienced a sense of notoriety from being a serial killer.

Jackson offered the following closing statement to the jury, "There are two people locked up in the body of this young giant:

one is fighting to be here with us now, and the other is slipping away to his world of violent fantasy where he is happy."

When he was found guilty, Edmund requested he be put to death. An ironic request, given that dying by the gas chamber was a game that he used to play with his sisters.

His request was denied, given that California had temporarily banned the death penalty at the time of his sentencing.

X

Solace Amid the Cement and Steel

THE TRIAL WAS OVER IN LESS THAN THREE weeks. After five hours of deliberation, the jury found Edmund guilty of eight counts of first-degree murder and sentenced him to life in prison at the California Medical Facility State Prison, in the small town of Vacaville. He shared the same cell block with Charles Manson and convicted killer Herbert Mullin.

Edmund did not show up for his parole hearings; he was eligible in 2007 and 2012, and declined both hearings. His attorney, Scott Currey, states, "His feeling is that he—and this is his belief—no one's ever going to let him out and he's happy; happy going about his life in prison."

For Edmund, prison is the only real home he has ever known; a safe place where his needs are taken care of. He is free from the murderous temptations he had experienced when he was around women and excised his past with his mother.

He is considered a model prisoner and involved in numerous activities, including crafting ceramic cups, scheduling the psychiatric appointments of other inmates, and recording audiobooks for the blind; he has completed over five thousand hours of narration.

Edmund has accommodated researchers by allowing them to interview him in their pursuit to better understand the minds of serial killers. In fact, he was one of the first murderers to be interviewed by the FBI's newly formed Behavioral Science Unit.

He feels he can provide a unique service to others by sharing his own experience in the hopes it can help someone else by preventing them from killing.

Edmund was one of the killers interviewed in the documentary *Murder: No Apparent Motive*, where he stated:

> *"There's somebody out there watching this and hasn't done that—hasn't killed people, and wants to, and rages inside*

and struggles with that feeling, or is so sure they have it under control. They need to talk to somebody about it. Trust somebody enough to sit down and talk about something that isn't a crime; thinking that way isn't a crime. Doing it isn't just a crime, it's a horrible thing, it doesn't know when to quit and it can't be stopped easily once it starts."

Despite the fact that Edmund is now a model prisoner, it was not always that way. There was an incident in the late 1970s when Edmund challenged a researcher, which resulted in a change in FBI policy.

Robert Ressler was a criminal profiler for the FBI, who had interviewed Edmund several times as part of the Criminal Personality Research Project he was working on. For his last interview with Edmund, Robert declined all offers by prison officials to have a guard present, which is normally provided for the security of visitors.

Robert felt comfortable with Edmund and felt any added security would interfere with the interview; besides, there was a button in the interviewing room that would alert guards if needed.

When the interview was over, Robert pushed the button so they could let him out of the locked room, but no guards came.

Robert pushed the button two more times, but to no avail. Edmund told him, "Relax. They're changing the shift, feeding the guys in the secure areas. Might be fifteen, twenty minutes before they come and get you." Robert was worried, which fed Edmund's manipulative personality. "If I went ape shit in here, you'd be in a lot of trouble, wouldn't you? I could screw your head off and place it on the table to greet the guard."

Robert tried to call Edmund's bluff by advising him of the potential consequences that he would incur if he harmed him, to which he replied, "What would they do—cut off my TV privileges?"

Understanding the futility of his response to Edmund, Robert told him he was carrying a weapon. Edmund inquired as to the kind of weapon he was carrying, but Robert told him he would not give specifics. His continued stalling bought him the time he needed for a guard to finally show up. As Robert left the room, Edmund told him, "You know I was just kidding, don't you?"

Since that incident, it has been FBI policy to conduct interviews with serial killers in pairs.

Edmund has also been known to manipulate other prisoners, in particular, Mullin. Edmund had a strong dislike for Mullin, who committed murders in Santa Cruz around the same time he did. He feels Mullin was an indiscriminate killer, with no good reason for what he did. At the same time, Edmund admits to the hypocrisy of his thinking. It was this kind of self-awareness that led FBI profiler John E. Douglas to call Edmund, "among the brightest prison inmates" he has ever interviewed, saying that he offered unique insights for a violent criminal.

Edmund used his towering six-foot nine-inch stature to impose his "house rules" on the five-foot-seven Mullin, whom he called "Herbie." Edmund could not stand it when Mullin sang while he and other prisoners were watching television.

Mullin liked to sing, but lacked any consideration for others. Edmund trained Mullin to be courteous to others by employing behavior modification. When Mullin distracted others with his singing, Edmund poured water on him. When he demonstrated courtesy by respecting others, Edmund gave him peanuts, one of his favorite treats.

Edmund's notoriety has made his story prominent in popular culture, inspiring movies, books, and music. In the 2000 film

American Psycho, Edmund is the inspiration for actor Christian Bale's character, Patrick Bateman, who uses some of Edmund's words as dialogue.

The 2008 cult horror film *Kemper: The Co-Ed Killer*, is loosely based on the facts of the case. Edmund was one of five serial killers used to develop the character of Buffalo Bill in the novel, *The Silence of the Lambs*.

In his 1996 novel *Intensity*, author Dean Koontz used Edmund as his inspiration for creating the character of Edgler Vess. Punk and Thrash metal bands have written songs about Edmund with titles like *Edmund Kemper had a Horrible Temper* by Macabre, *Fortress* by System of a Down, and *Murder* by the German duo, Seabound.

Accessories can be purchased online that bear his image include: t-shirts, trading cards, novelty coins, and tote bags.

Even though Edmund Kemper has been denied parole multiple times, his family still lives in fear that one day he will be granted parole through some fluke.

Jeffrey Dahmer

The Gruesome True Story of a Hungry Cannibalistic Rapist and Necrophiliac Serial Killer

Introduction

A PLANET WITH A POPULATION OF OVER SEVEN billion is bound to produce moments of greatness. These are events, which, for better or for worse, mark the course of humanity and change it forever.

Throughout the existence of humankind, we have witnessed and recorded these moments: destructive wars, terrible disasters, heroic last stands, heartwarming acts, the creation of impressive structures, and amazing adventures.

Earth has seen it all, and it has learned from these moments in time.

All these moments have something in common. Individuals, equally great men and women, whose names remain in our history and our memories forever, brought these moments to life.

There are people whose names we remember for the good they brought to the world; they made our planet a better place while here, and we sorely miss them when they are gone. Some well-known people are more controversial than others—some are hated—while others are loved. These include conquerors, kings, queens, and perhaps even rock stars; one way or another, these famous people had an impact on our history.

The following book will not discuss such characters.

No. The subject of this book is not just a man shrouded in greatness—great evil that is—but also one who did not leave goodness behind him after his death. He left no positive legacy, nor lessons for the people who knew him to learn. His name strikes terror and disgust in those who hear it, and anybody who was ever around him still trembles in fear at the mention of his name.

Every so often, humanity spawns monsters—beasts disguised by human skin—who care little for their fellow beings and wish only to satisfy their own needs. These are killers, rapists, torturers, and other criminals who are spawned from the dark, to bring pain and distress to those around them.

Even then, some are more ruthless and despicable than others in this group. There are big names—celebrities of murder, so to speak—even among those who cause pain.

This book is about one of the biggest of these names—a monster that is known worldwide and feared universally.

The subject of the following book is a man who brought pain and suffering to a large number of victims. He never felt a shred of pity or remorse for what he had done or the way his actions ruined the lives of the many families and friends of those he killed.

This killer took seventeen lives: seventeen victims who did not go quietly.

The man who killed these poor souls saw them simply as 'things.' They were objects to pleasure him as he raped and brutalized them, watching intently as their lives seeped out of their bodies.

His name, of course, is **Jeffrey Dahmer**. This monster, known as the Milwaukee Cannibal, was a killer who began to hurt living beings as early as childhood. Dahmer enjoyed every second of his murders—from the abductions, the preservation, and even the consumption of his victims.

Yet, the biggest issue with Dahmer was not necessarily what he did, but the fact that he was *good at it*, and could not bring himself to stop.

Now is the moment for you to discover the tale of one of America's worst killers. If you are faint of heart, consider putting this book down to prepare yourself before starting to read; the grisly details will not be spared.

There is no shortage of material on Jeffrey Dahmer from various sources: books, magazines, even on the internet. However, this is not merely recounting his life story and the murders. Rather, it is a push into the abyss of Dahmer's mind. You see, this book will change you, for better or for worse.

The horrific tale of Jeffrey Dahmer and his murders is about to begin.

I

The Loss of Innocence

BEFORE WE BEGIN, THE FOLLOWING MUST BE
said, if only to separate our killer from other monsters — to
take away the possibility of doubt or pity. Jeffrey Dahmer, unlike
many others who have become serial killers, was not born into an
abusive household, nor forced into what he became by terrible
poverty and bad influences.

Jeffrey could have become whatever he wished, but he chose to
become a killer. And not just any killer: *One of the worst killers the
world has ever seen.*

Our story begins on the 21st of May in 1960. Jeffrey Lionel
Dahmer was born in West Allis, Wisconsin, to Joyce Annette and

Lionel Herbert Dahmer. Joyce was a teletype machine instructor, while Lionel studied analytical chemistry at Marquette University.

As a baby, Jeffrey received all the attention a child could wish for; his parents took good care of him. However, as the years passed and their marriage became tense, Lionel and Joyce began to somewhat neglect him. The disruption in the marriage was due in part to Joyce's personality. Being the type of person who continuously demanded attention, Joyce would go as far as faking sickness to get responsiveness.

It did not help that Lionel was very busy with his studies, spending extended periods of time away from home, only to return to his wife, feigning a nervous breakdown.

Despite initially being a happy and playful child, a change occurred after Jeffery underwent double hernia surgery at the age of six. He became quieter and more subdued.

In school, Jeffrey was considered to be a quiet and shy boy; he showed signs of neglect but had fortunately managed to make some friends. While there are claims that a neighbor molested Jeffrey at some point in his younger years, no one has confirmed these allegations. Dahmer himself later recalled having been present on several occasions when his parents argued. These scenes were upsetting for a child. Fortunately, Dahmer's parents' love for him did not change at any point.

As a young boy, Jeffrey fell completely in love with animals. The family had a pet dog, and, at one point, they helped nurse a bird back to health from an injury. Lionel would later recall Jeffrey watched the bird fly away into the wild with "wide, gleaming eyes," and it had probably been the happiest moment in his life.

Shortly after, Jeffrey came upon his father, sweeping some animal bones out from under their home. He felt intensely curious when he saw the body parts and asked his father what they were. Lionel noticed when Jeffrey heard the crunching noises the bones made, he seemed oddly thrilled, requesting to touch them himself. Later, Lionel would come to understand this was the very first sign of what his son would eventually become.

In 1966, Lionel graduated then found a job as a research chemist. Unfortunately for the family, this would require them to uproot and move to Akron, Ohio. Joyce was pregnant with their second son, David. Her pregnancy was a troublesome one, making her weak and prone to sickness. Jeffrey, now seven, gradually received less and less attention, and he began to lose self-confidence and his previously bubbly nature diminished.

Soon, even the very idea of starting a new school made Jeffrey fearful. Lionel tried not to worry, hoping Jeffrey had just not adapted to his new home yet. In reality, it was far more than that.

After buying and moving into a new home in April 1967, young Jeffrey seemed to begin to get used to his new life, even finding a new friend named Lee. Jeffrey also grew close to a female teacher, who he eventually gifted a bowl of tadpoles he had caught on his own. Later, however, he would find out his teacher had given the bowl to Lee. This event angered Jeffrey and led him to sneak into the boy's garage to poison the animals' water with motor oil, killing all of them.

This occasion was not the last time Jeffrey came into contact with dead animals.

The young Dahmer was fascinated with hunting his neighborhood for the corpses of critters. He often took them home and dissected them, sometimes getting rid of the bones in the woods near his home to avoid raising suspicion. When he went fishing with his father, Jeffrey's favorite part of the activity was cutting open the fish and gutting them. Nobody paid attention to this proclivity.

One night, during a family dinner of chicken, Jeffrey asked his father what would happen if he put the chicken bones in a bleach solution. His father, pleasantly surprised by his child's curiosity, decided to teach him how to bleach animal bones, safely and correctly. There was no harm in it, his father thought. After all, it was merely a childish curiosity. His father was most likely relieved by Jeffrey's request since he had shown such little interest in other hobbies up to this point.

Had someone known what was really happening, Dahmer's story may have ended very differently.

Jeffrey wasn't just inspecting the insides of animal corpses and preserving their bones for science.

He was getting ready for something much worse.

II

An Odd Young Man

JEFFREY'S HIGH SCHOOL YEARS ARRIVED, AND HE began to grow in stature. As a tall, awkward youth, he shifted from random quiet, shy states to extroverted ones. He developed a penchant for playing crude practical jokes when he was drunk; this habit would continue throughout the years up to Jeffrey's death.

Classmates stated that Dahmer would arrive to class looking disheveled, with a can or two of beer in his bag, to consume during class. A curious classmate once asked him why he was continuously drinking during class, to which Dahmer responded: "It's my medicine."

His jokes were cruel. He often mimicked his mother's interior designer, who had cerebral palsy, to the enjoyment of many of his peers. Other times he would paint chalk outlines in the halls of his school, reminiscent of those found at crime scenes once law enforcement removed the body.

Jeffrey was considered to be intelligent and polite but regularly received average grades due to his extreme apathy and lack of interest in studying or reading. His parents hired a private tutor, but nothing changed. Dahmer was not willing to make an effort, so there was little the tutor could do.

It was around this age that Dahmer discovered two important things that would define him as a human being and mold him into what he would become later.

The first was that he was gay. Jeffrey first noticed it as a small attraction towards other men, but even in these early stages of realization, Dahmer kept it from his parents. He had a brief relationship with another boy, but it did not get very far.

Then he had a second, separate realization. Dahmer began to fantasize about dominating another male, taking complete control, doing whatever he wanted to a partner, without their consent.

Jeffrey wanted to hurt somebody, to make sexual use of them, and perhaps kill and dissect them in the process. The limits of sex and dissection began to blur, as Dahmer included one within the other in his fantasies. His desire for violence became so overwhelming, and he began to make plans for his first victim.

The idea that would finally spark Jeffrey's killer instinct came to fruition. On several occasions, Dahmer had spotted a male jogger he found attractive. He knew the man's route passed by a section of thick bushes. Dahmer had the perfect place to hide, as well as the perfect opportunity to take advantage of his victim if he could successfully render him unconscious.

After fantasizing about this idea, Dahmer decided to make his fantasy come true. Armed with a baseball bat, he went to the bushes and lay in wait, patiently expecting the jogger. To the man's extreme good fortune, he did not jog that route on that particular day, and Dahmer decided to give up on his fantasy. If the would-be victim had passed through the bushy area, Dahmer almost certainly would have followed through with his plan.

In the Dahmer household, Lionel and Joyce's marriage was deteriorating. The couple had less and less patience for each other. Arguments were becoming a regular event, and Jeffrey was having a hard time seeing them fight. His drinking increased; he became more despondent as time passed.

Jeffrey's terrible and secret habit of dissecting and skinning animals became the only thing that motivated him. His parents and other grown-ups watched as his peers spoke of dreams, careers, and plans, while Dahmer sunk further into apathy and purposelessness. Jeffrey was more comfortable lying on his bed alone in his room than making an effort in his studies or looking for a job. At this point, even interacting with other people had become a challenge for him.

Even worse, nobody could detect what Jeffrey was truly harboring on the inside because of his guarded and closed nature. He did not argue with anyone, never got involved in his parents' increasingly common fights, and kept his strange habits secret enough for everyone to find him merely different—not actually troubled or sick

When Jeffrey was almost eighteen, his parents finally gave up on their marriage and got divorced. Where Joyce had been a self-centered woman with barely any attention for Jeffrey, Lionel's new fiancée, Shari, was more attentive toward the boy. She recommended that Jeffrey start college after high school, and Lionel agreed.

It looked like Jeffrey was going to turn over a new leaf. He seemed as though he might get an education that could help him progress as a human being. Jeffrey had a chance to start over and become a regular person, despite his awkward teenage years and childhood.

Unfortunately, Jeffrey's fate was about to darken. He was about to let loose the demon who inhabited his mind. Jeffrey Dahmer was about to become the killer the world would remember; the construction of a horrific legacy was about to begin.

III

A Taste of Blood

JEFFREY GRADUATED FROM HIGH SCHOOL IN THE summer of 1978. He was now eighteen years old. Lionel Dahmer had gone on a business trip with his new wife, while Jeffrey's mother, Joyce, and younger brother, David, had relocated to Wisconsin.

Jeffrey was left alone at home with his dark thoughts and darker desires. It was just a matter of time before he acted on them.

It wouldn't take long.

Just three weeks after graduating, with nobody around to supervise him or give him a moment of pause before making a rash decision—that he would never be able to take back, Jeffrey Dahmer took his first life.

Eighteen-year-old Steven Mark Hicks would become Dahmer's first victim. Dahmer had imagined picking up a male hitchhiker and killing him. Not only did he have the freedom to do so, but as it happened, Hicks was hitchhiking as Dahmer was out looking for someone to fulfill his fantasy.

After exchanging a few words, Jeffrey invited Hicks to his home for some beers. Steven agreed, unaware that Dahmer wanted to unleash his macabre desires on him.

When the two arrived at Dahmer's home, he pulled out some alcohol from the fridge, put some rock music on the radio, and began enjoying Hicks' company.

However, at some point in the conversation, Dahmer realized that Steven was not gay like himself. There was an awkward exchange, at which Steven said he wanted to go home. Dahmer thought he had heard wrong. *Go home?* Why would his victim want to go home? This request was awkward for Dahmer; he had so many things in mind for the night. Hicks was about to ruin it all by leaving.

Something snapped in Dahmer's mind. He approached Steven from behind while he was sitting down. Dahmer held a ten-pound dumbbell in his hand. Hicks had no time to react as Dahmer slammed the heavy object into his head twice, knocking him unconscious.

However, the bludgeoning was not the end of the attack. Dahmer knelt over Steven's body, strangling him to death with the bar of his rudimentary weapon. Then he stripped the fresh corpse of its clothes and masturbated over it with sick pleasure.

Jeffrey Dahmer had finally acted on his fantasies, and the sensation felt strange. While part of him wanted to weep over what he had done, another part was glad that he had finally followed through on years of dark fantasies. It was a mix of emotions. Dahmer was not in a hurry to kill again... yet.

The next day, Dahmer was finally able to put into practice what he had been learning for years. Dragging the body downstairs to a crawl space, he dissected it and buried the remains in a shallow grave in his backyard. Several weeks later, he would exhume the body parts, remove the flesh from the bones, dissolve it in acid, and flush the remaining solution down the toilet.

Six weeks later, Lionel and Shari returned home. They found Jeffrey home alone—doing nothing productive with his life. He agreed to enroll at Ohio State University, majoring in business.

Initially, his father had high hopes for his son. However, Dahmer wasted no time proving he was not going to stop abusing alcohol anytime soon. With no accomplishments at the University, he quit before even completing his first term. Dahmer was back slouching around at home.

Lionel would not tolerate Jeffrey's apathy. If he was not going to study, there was space in the Army for him. In January 1979, Jeffrey Dahmer enlisted in the U.S. Army. He trained to become a medical specialist at Fort Sam, Houston. Considered an effective soldier, he was stationed in Baumholder, West Germany, a few months later.

Once there, Dahmer fulfilled the role of a combat medic. It was not the ideal position for him since he could not stand looking at blood, a strange detail that psychologists would later explain as guilt over Steven Hick's murder, but Dahmer tried his best to perform the required duties.

While the Army officially recorded his performance as a soldier as being "average or above average," there were some ugly rumors about Dahmer, that in retrospect, chill the blood.

In 2010, one soldier said that Dahmer had repeatedly raped him during a seventeen-month period, while another stated he had been drugged and raped by Dahmer in an armored vehicle in 1979.

Alcoholism and loneliness continued to drag Dahmer down, and he was eventually declared unfit for service. The Army formally and honorably discharged him in March 1981. Not long after, Dahmer was sent to Fort Jackson for debriefing. As part of his release from service, the military subsequently provided Dahmer with a ticket to a destination of his choice, anywhere in the country.

Deciding where to go was tough for Dahmer. Ultimately, he felt he had disappointed his father too much to return to Ohio. He did not want to return there with his tail between his legs. Determined to live by his own means, Dahmer chose to travel to Miami Beach, Florida, where he got a job at a sandwich place. Nobody would have guessed that the tall young man preparing their lunch was a killer, who would soon go on to become legendary among murderers.

Dahmer's alcoholism was ever-present, despite having a stable job. However, Jeffrey found himself unable to keep up with his responsibilities. His landlord evicted him for missing rent payments. Now the young man knew he only had one person to turn to, so he called his father, asking if he could return to live with him in Ohio. Lionel accepted.

Coming home was a source of simultaneous comfort and discomfort for Dahmer. While his return allowed him to walk around familiar territory, it also reminded him of what he had done to Steven Hicks; one detail nagged at him, causing him to worry about getting caught.

As soon as he had the chance to be home alone, Dahmer unearthed the bones he had buried in his father's backyard and took a sledgehammer to them, pulverizing the body parts completely and scattering them in the woodlands behind the family home.

As Dahmer disposed of the bones, he hoped that his murder experimentation had ended—that he would recover from his dark fantasies. Unfortunately for both him and future victims, he had only temporarily quashed these dreams of control, pain, and murder.

In fact, they would all come flooding back at any moment…

IV

No Escaping Who You Are

ONLY THREE WEEKS AFTER HAVING RETURNED to Ohio, in October 1981, Jeffrey messed up again, frustrating his father and stepmother tenfold.

After drinking too much, Jeffrey was arrested for drunken and disorderly conduct. Lionel was not as forgiving as on previous occasions. He and his wife decided Jeffrey had to go elsewhere to truly start over.

While he had mostly been a cold, quiet boy during his life, Jeffrey had shown to carry an affection for his grandmother, Lionel's mother. Lionel hoped that Jeffrey could start over at her home in

West Allis, Wisconsin—thinking a change of scenery could help Jeffrey become more responsible and mature.

Moving to West Allis, Jeffrey Dahmer immediately adapted to a new, calmer life than the one experienced in both Ohio and Florida. His grandmother paid more attention to his behavior than his parents ever had. He accompanied her to many activities and helped her out with a variety of chores. His only trouble obeying his grandmother was with quitting alcohol, but professionally, his life took a general turn for the better. He even found a decent job at a blood plasma center, where he helped collect blood from donors.

Meanwhile, Dahmer's personal life continued to decline. His behavior became increasingly stranger, worrying his grandmother. At one point, she entered Jeffrey's room and was shocked to find a fully-dressed male mannequin in his closet. He had been using it as a sex toy of some kind. She also discovered a .357 Magnum under his bed. The elderly woman was not sure if he was capable of using the firearm because Dahmer had never shown her his violent side. Eventually, she would ask Dahmer to throw it away.

In 1982, Dahmer was arrested for indecent exposure in front of a crowd of over twenty-five women and children. He was convicted and fined fifty dollars, plus court costs. Lionel was always there to pay whatever costs were generated by Dahmer's mistakes. Time and again, he crossed his fingers, hoping his son would change his ways. Interestingly, this undying hope became a recurring pattern that Lionel repeated even after Jeffrey was caught. He had a warm heart when it came to his son, despite the constant disappointments.

In January 1985, Dahmer gained employment as a mixer at the Milwaukee Ambrosia Chocolate Factory, where he worked eight hours, at nine dollars an hour, six nights a week. He enjoyed the job and the freedom that came with it. Around this time, he visited the West Allis Public Library, spending some of his time off reading books and newspaper articles.

His dark fantasies were reignited there.

While at the library one day, a man walked past Dahmer and lay a note on his table, offering to perform fellatio on Dahmer. Despite Dahmer not answering the man's note, it aroused him. He recalled the fantasies of being in control and dominant.

Consequently, Dahmer started to actively seek out sexual partners at gay bars, bookstores, and bathhouses in the area, trying to find men interested in fulfilling his desires. Ultimately, he preferred the bathhouses for their added privacy, increased intimacy, and a relaxing atmosphere.

First, Dahmer used the bathhouses to find consensual sexual partners but soon began to feel uncomfortable and frustrated when his lovers moved and made noises while he was pleasuring them. As previously stated, Dahmer required total control and dominance; acts of sexual intercourse were no different. From Dahmer's perspective, other men were simply objects of pleasure, not people. As a result, he thought of ways to reduce the influence that a partner had during sex and began to purchase sleeping pills.

Dahmer engaged in consensual acts of intercourse until June 1986, where his curiosity overwhelmed him, and he began to drug his victims by lacing their beverages with sedatives. Then he took advantage of their bodies, raping them with no regard for their comfort or consent. This pattern occurred a dozen times until the bathhouse's administration grew wary of him and revoked his membership. Additionally, they barred Dahmer from ever entering the bathhouse again. However, no one pressed charges, so Jeffrey Dahmer simply walked away from his violent crimes without consequence.

Around this time, Dahmer read in the newspaper about the funeral of an eighteen-year-old male, who had recently died and been buried. He saw the boy's picture and imagined himself raping the corpse, which aroused him. He visited the grave one night with a spade and began to dig, but found the soil too hard to penetrate and decided to abort his plan.

That same year, police arrested Dahmer again for indecent exposure. He was caught masturbating in front of two boys, near the Kinnickinnic River, in August. The police brought him into the station for questioning. Although he initially admitted he had been pleasuring himself, he later changed the story to state that he was only urinating when witnesses spotted him. The prosecution changed the charges to disorderly conduct and the court sentenced Dahmer to a one-year probation, as well as a series of counseling visits.

Law enforcement had already arrested Dahmer twice, and yet again, nobody recognized his sinister capacity. This oversight continued to occur on further occasions, with family members, neighbors, and even law enforcement officers failing to see beyond his quiet, shy façade, to spot the monster lurking behind. The real Dahmer, for all his fantasies and one murder victim already to his name, was invisible to everyone around him.

Jeffrey's murderous tendencies had been dormant for years, but a mixture of factors had reawakened his true nature and brought out his urges again. His ability to blend in, coupled with Dahmer's blatant disregard for getting caught, acted as a useful tactic for him.

It was one that would soon come in handy when, once again, he began to kill.

V

Reawakened

NINE YEARS.

It had been over nine years since 1978 when Dahmer had killed hitchhiker Steven Hicks. In the interim, Dahmer had drugged and raped men, been arrested twice for indecent exposure, yet he had not killed again.

Unfortunately, this grace period was approaching its end.

Dahmer regularly brought partners home to his grandmother's house in West Allis, to have sex. However, on one occasion in November 1987, after having his bathhouse permit revoked, Dahmer visited a gay bar in search of someone to take to a hotel.

There, he met twenty-five-year-old Steven Tuomi from Michigan, and sadly he would become Dahmer's second murder victim.

Dahmer stated that he had only intended to drug Steven, rape him while he was unconscious, and then part ways with him the next morning, never to see him again.

However, events did not go as planned.

According to Dahmer, he awoke the next morning to find Tuomi lying under him; the man's chest had caved in and was heavily bruised. Dahmer's own forearm was also very bruised, his fists bloody. Dahmer states he sat there in shock, looking at the corpse, and his own hands, trying to find an explanation. He claimed he did not remember killing Tuomi and stuck with this story to his grave, never confessing to committing the murder.

In fact, Dahmer always argued he did not remember anything about the night of Tuomi's death. He explained when he woke to find Tuomi dead, only one thing mattered to him—getting rid of the corpse. Dahmer had registered the hotel room in his own name and realized detection would mean getting locked up for real.

Dahmer left the hotel briefly to purchase a large suitcase, which he used to store Tuomi's body in, before calling a cab. Successfully avoiding detection in the hotel's lobby, Dahmer checked out and walked to the taxi waiting for him. The driver helped him get the suitcase into the vehicle.

To which the taxi driver complained about the weight, asking, "What's in here, a corpse?"

Jeffrey Dahmer smiled knowingly and nodded, and the driver finished putting the suitcase in the car before setting off to Dahmer's grandmother's home.

The corpse remained in his grandmother's basement for an entire week, during which time Dahmer had sex with it, masturbated on it, and finally began to dismember it to dispose of the evidence. He began by severing the head, arms, and legs from the torso, before filleting the bones from the body and dicing the flesh into small pieces. He moved the flesh to garbage bags, while the bones were placed in a sheet and ground into splinters with the same sledgehammer he had used for his first victim's body. Two hours later, Dahmer had destroyed Steven Tuomi's remains completely, except for the victim's head.

For a while, Dahmer kept Tuomi's head as a trophy, storing it in a blanket. Then he boiled and treated it with a mix of industrial detergent and bleach to preserve the skull. His obsession with bones had never truly gone away, and now he used the skull as stimulation for arousal and masturbation. It eventually grew too brittle to manipulate, and Dahmer was forced to take his sledgehammer to it and throw the remains away. Law enforcement officials never found them.

While he had previously felt guilty for killing Steven Hicks, Dahmer did not feel the same about Tuomi. Confused? Perhaps. Certainly, not guilty, however. He had even had some fun disposing of the body. His beloved grandmother was none the wiser.

Tuomi's murder buoyed Dahmer's previously-dwindling desire to kill. Now, he began actively searching for victims. Visiting gay bars, he used his established method: offer his victims money to pose for photographs, or simply have a drink and watch some movies with him at home—before actually taking them to his grandmother's, strangling them after drugging and raping them. Just like while they were living, he considered male corpses sexual objects. He often penetrated and masturbated on them. Dahmer also kept trophies from the victims' bodies, thinking of the skull as the most important body part a victim could leave him.

Steven Tuomi was the last murder victim that Dahmer disposed of quickly and without much fuss. The reality is, Jeffrey

Dahmer was not an 'average' or a simple killer. Whereas the actual process of hunting a victim and taking their life is the thrill for most murderers, to Dahmer, this was only the prelude to the joyous experience which came after.

Similar to other serial killers, with control and domination forces pushing Dahmer to continue killing, He differed significantly in that he was not interested in hearing a victim beg, or watching them despair as he cut or killed them. He ended lives quickly, was very subtle in his intentions, and even helped them to go more 'easily' by drugging them.

In truth, Dahmer was more of a necrophiliac than anything else; he just took things a step further by creating the corpses for himself.

Two months after murdering Steven Tuomi, Dahmer met James Doxtator, a fourteen-year-old, who was working as a male sex worker. Dahmer lured the boy to his home with an offer of fifty dollars, to take some nude photographs.

James was only a child, Dahmer would soon add him to his growing pile of the dead.

The killing spree was about to begin.

VI

Killing Spree

DOXTATOR WAS YOUNG AND NAÏVE. HE WENT to Dahmer's West Allis residence without a second thought. There, he and Dahmer had sex, and the murderer then drugged the boy. While James was sedated, Dahmer strangled him on the floor of his grandmother's cellar.

Dahmer left the corpse alone for a week before dismembering it, having used the body as a source of sexual stimulation and masturbating on it regularly. He disposed of the body parts in the trash, separating the skull from the rest and keeping it. He boiled it in the same solution he had used with Tuomi. Dahmer kept the skull for a while before using his sledgehammer to pulverize it.

Dahmer's next victim was twenty-two-year-old Richard Guerrero, a bisexual man he met outside a gay bar on March 24, 1988.

Dahmer may have been a shy young man during his teenage years, but when he wanted to lure a victim to their death, he was quite outgoing. All it took was an offer of fifty dollars and a night of sex to get Richard to follow him home. They were soon on their way to Dahmer's grandmother's house. There, Dahmer used a leather strap to strangle the life out of a sedated Guerrero, who had a drink laced with sleeping pills. Just like that, Dahmer had taken the lives of four men. This time, he felt immediately aroused at seeing Guerrero's corpse and began to perform oral sex on the body.

Twenty-four hours later, Dahmer dismembered the man's corpse, separated the skull to keep as a trophy. It would remain in Dahmer's possession for several more months until he decided to pulverize it with his sledgehammer.

On April 23, 1988, just one month after killing Guerrero, Dahmer struck again. He lured a young man from a gay bar to his grandmother's home and invited him in for coffee. The beverage contained several sleeping pills, which Dahmer used to sedate the man, just as he had done with his previous victims. However, as

Dahmer waited for the drugs to take their effect, he heard his grandmother moving around in the room above them.

"Is that you, Jeff?" she called out. Dahmer awkwardly replied that he was alone, but correctly guessed that his grandmother did not believe him. He decided not to take any risks and was left frustrated as his victim lost consciousness. Dahmer did not hurt, rape, or murder the young man, instead choosing to take him to County General Hospital before returning home.

Dahmer continued to bring men to his grandmother's home, although without killing anyone else, for an extended period. Eventually, this arrangement became unacceptable to her. She had already expressed her discomfort with strangers being in her home, as well as the horrible smells that regularly came up from the cellar.

On one occasion, she even found a strange black sticky substance on the cellar floor, emitting a foul smell. Jeffrey's only answer was he had been experimenting on animals, and left it at that. But his grandmother had finally had enough, and at the beginning of September 1988, she asked her grandson to find a new place to live.

Dahmer did not take long to find a place.

His new home was a one-bedroom apartment, where he moved on September 25th.

Then, only twenty-four hours later, Dahmer made one of the biggest mistakes of his life.

Whatever poison was eating away at Dahmer's mind was not restricted to just murdering innocent men or defiling their bodies; it also involved a sexual attraction to minors—a troublesome fact for Dahmer, due to how society views child molesters and sex offenders.

However, it did not stop Dahmer from going ahead with his plans anyway.

Just one day after moving to his new home, Dahmer approached thirteen-year-old Somsack Sinthasomphone, in an attempt to take nude photographs of him. Even though the child agreed to go back home with Dahmer, later, he went to the police to report the murderer for having drugged and fondled him while he had been sedated. The killer had crushed sleeping pills and put them in Irish Cream, but they had only started to take full effect when the boy had arrived home. His father realized what had happened after interrogating his son.

Consequently, in January 1989, Dahmer was convicted of second-degree sexual assault and enticing a child for immoral purposes. The court suspended sentencing until May.

In March, while Dahmer awaited sentencing, he moved back to his grandmother's home. Ironically, despite the ax hanging over his head and the family's shock over what he had done, Dahmer still found time to kill again.

Dahmer's fifth victim was twenty-four-year-old biracial model Anthony Sears, who Dahmer met at a gay bar on March 25, 1989. Later Dahmer would state he had been at the bar merely to pass the time, with no intention of murdering anybody.

Unfortunately for Sears, he approached Dahmer with an innocent curiosity—exactly what Dahmer could not resist and used to his advantage. As Dahmer remembers, it was shortly before the bar closed, when Sears simply began talking to him. Dahmer found him exceptionally attractive. After a chat, Dahmer invited the man home—in spite of his grandmother forbidding him to do so. The two men performed oral sex on one another in the basement. Then Dahmer drugged and strangled Sears, repeating the tried and tested murder method he had used on his previous victims.

To dispose of his victim's body, Dahmer placed the corpse in his grandmother's bathtub and decapitated it, before unsuccessfully attempting to flay it. Eventually, he resorted to his typical method: stripping the flesh with a mix of potent chemical substances and pulverizing the bones soon after. He kept Sears' genitalia, as well as the man's head, and preserved them in acetone. They would be two of his most prized possessions for a long time.

The big day arrived on May 23, 1989. Dahmer's lawyer Gerald Boyle and Assistant District Attorney Gale Shelton faced off with attempts to defend and lock away the criminal, respectively. Both were unaware he was a serial killer. Shelton argued Dahmer did not appear to understand the full extent of his crimes, only seeing his actions as wrong because his victim was too young, rather than recognizing it was far more about the gravity of the act of drugging and sexual abuse. According to Shelton, this fact made Dahmer a dangerous individual. The D.A. wanted Dahmer put away in prison for at least five years, a sentence that would allow him to reflect properly on his crimes. Studies from psychologists supported this theory, demonstrating Dahmer was a manipulative and evasive character, who required intensive treatment.

Meanwhile, Boyle argued treatment was indeed needed, but without prison time. He cited on the positive side, Dahmer had kept his job and there was some normalcy in his life. He also emphasized Dahmer was not a multiple offender. Again, it is an example of the unawareness Jeffrey had killed five human beings by now—they had caught him before he had gone too far. To Boyle, "It was a blessing in disguise that Dahmer had been caught."

Dahmer was given a chance to defend himself; he was quick to lay the blame for his crimes on alcoholism. His manner of speaking convinced those in the courtroom. Dahmer made sure to act shocked, disappointed for what he had done, and repentant. He reiterated to the courtroom he had been able to keep a stable job and asked the judge and jury not to take this away from him. He said he wanted, "A chance to get help to turn his life around."

Safe to say, everyone was convinced. The judge stayed Dahmer's sentence and put him on probation instead of sending him straight to prison. He was also ordered to spend one year in the Milwaukee County House of Correction, under a "work release" regime. This allowed him to work during the day and return to jail at night. However, he was required to register as a sex offender. Jeffrey Dahmer was no longer as invisible as he wished to be.

During this time, Lionel was heavily involved in helping him out with legal costs and support. He still had faith in his son's recovery and yet another chance to start over. In Lionel's mind, Jeffrey was a "child who had slipped beyond his grasp, a little boy that was spinning in the void, swirling in the maelstrom, lost, lost, lost." He even openly opposed Jeffrey's premature release from the House of Correction, arguing that his son needed to be fully treated before he could harm others—and himself—even more.

The justice system ignored Lionel, the man who understood Jeffrey better than anyone else. Many innocent men would pay the price with their lives.

It had yet to be determined whether Jeffrey was a man who had suffered as a child and grown corrupt or was a terrible monster that took pleasure in defiling his fellow human beings. Nonetheless, confirmation was coming quickly.

Dahmer soon moved to another residence of his own. He would continue his murders into the year 1990.

The Milwaukee Cannibal was about to earn his name...

...in the worst possible way.

VII

Lost in The Maelstrom

AS PREVIOUSLY MENTIONED, DAHMER DID NOT fully complete his treatment upon his release; the judge granted him early release for good behavior. Dahmer, only ten months later, was a free man. Lionel even tried to stop this premature release by sending a letter requesting his son receive his complete treatment—for Jeffrey's own good—but the justice system ignored his pleas.

Dahmer found his way back into his grandmother's home by March of 1990, but once again, she asked him to find a place of his own to live.

That is how Jeffrey Dahmer ended up at his infamous address; Apartment 213, 924 North 25th Street. At Apartment 213, was where the most terrible part of Dahmer's story would occur; where Dahmer's monstrous nature would be revealed to the nation and world, once he was captured.

Dahmer took home his sixth victim just one week after moving in. The frequency of his murders was about to explode; he would end up killing men as often as once a week.

The latest man to become one of Dahmer's trophies was thirty-two-year-old Raymond Smith. He was a sex worker, who Dahmer lured to his apartment with the promise of fifty dollars for sex—a recurring trap in this tale.

Raymond accepted a drink from Dahmer without a second thought; if only he had known there were seven sleeping pills dissolved in the beverage. As soon as the effects of sedation kicked in, Dahmer strangled the man with his bare hands and took advantage of his corpse.

The next day, Dahmer went out and purchased a Polaroid camera. Returning home, he found a new use for his victim's corpse: posing Smith's body suggestively using it as a stimulus for masturbation.

After he finished taking the Polaroids, Dahmer dismembered the body in his bathroom. He boiled the arms, legs, and pelvis with Soilex—an industrial detergent—and then rinsed the bones in a sink. Jeffrey then separated the skull from the body, dissolving the rest of the skeleton in a container filled with acid. Keeping the skull as a trophy, Dahmer spray-painted it and stored it with Anthony Sears' skull, which he had brought with him from his previous address.

Just one week later, on May 27, Dahmer found his next victim. He lured a young man to his home, after having met him at a gay bar. Once there, however, Dahmer made a mistake; he accidentally consumed the drink he had laced with sedatives for his victim and ended up falling into a deep sleep. By the time he awoke the next day, the nameless young man had stolen several items and cash from him, but Dahmer never reported the incident to the police.

The next month, Dahmer lured a friend of his, twenty-seven-year-old Edward Smith, to his apartment. He drugged Smith and strangled the life out of him before wondering about the best way to preserve his corpse. Dahmer had already used bleaching techniques, but that weakened the bones and skull and made them brittle.

He decided to put the skeleton in his freezer for several months, hoping it would avoid moisture. Eventually, Dahmer realized the freezer did not stop the moisture-retention of the bones, and consequently was forced to dissolve the skeleton in acid. He placed the skull in his oven to dry, but it exploded suddenly and violently, becoming a useless mound of dust.

Dahmer later admitted he had felt terrible about killing someone 'pointlessly,' since he was unable to retain the man's body parts. In Dahmer's view, Edward Smith practically "did not count" for his personal record. No one was ever able to locate any of Smith's remains.

Three months after the murder of Edward Smith, Dahmer picked up twenty-two-year-old Ernest Miller. He met Miller on the corner of a street, luring him home with his typical offer of fifty dollars for his companionship. Dahmer asked Miller to let him listen to his heart and stomach, and he agreed. When Jeffrey prompted Miller for oral sex, Miller told Dahmer it would cost him a bit more.

Dahmer offered him a drink before they continued, and found he only had two sleeping pills remaining in his cupboard. Two pills would not be enough to sedate an adult male properly, so Dahmer would have to improvise. After watching Miller take the drink and then begin showing signs of sedation, Dahmer pulled out a knife and slashed his carotid artery open. The victim, visibly shocked, bled out within minutes. Dahmer went and picked up his Polaroid camera, taking pictures of Miller's dead body in several poses, before placing it in his bathtub.

Next, he severed the corpse's head. Later, Dahmer admitted to kissing and talking to the head during the dismemberment process. Dahmer removed the victim's heart, biceps, and other fleshy parts from the skeleton and stored them in his fridge in plastic bags. The terrible truth is that Dahmer wanted to consume the body parts later. He boiled the remaining flesh and organs with Soilex and rinsed the skeleton with the intention of preserving and keeping it as a trophy.

He bleached the victim's bones—the trick he had learned from an unknowing Lionel in his childhood—then painted and coated it with enamel, before placing it into the fridge.

Around this time, neighbors of 924 North 25th Street began complaining of foul odors coming from Jeffrey Dahmer's apartment. The building's landlord confronted Dahmer, and he apologized, stating he had a broken fridge and would get it fixed as soon as possible.

The lie served him well, and Dahmer did not have further trouble with the people in his building after that. Even so, some neighbors remained curious about the sounds of heavy falling objects, as well as the random hours at which a power saw could be heard coming from Dahmer's apartment.

Between September and October 1990, Dahmer met a twenty-two-year-old father, David Thomas, at a mall. He offered money in exchange for a few drinks, and a bit more if he agreed to pose for photographs. David was not aware of the photographs that Dahmer planned to take were of his corpse, so he agreed. Once at home, Dahmer provided Thomas with his special concoction, from which Thomas fell asleep soon after.

Once Thomas was out cold, Dahmer looked at him more closely and realized he had no attraction toward the man. He had suddenly lost interest in raping him. Dahmer began to think of what to do, but ultimately decided that letting Thomas re-awaken was too much of a risk; he strangled the man and dismembered his corpse. While dismembering him, Dahmer recorded the entire process with photographs and retained them, although he discarded all of the body parts.

Police would later show the pictures to Thomas's sister, who was forced to go through the ordeal of attempting to identify her brother.

Five months passed before Dahmer killed again. A dark cloud passed through his mind and his life. Suddenly, he began to fail at what he did best—charming men to lure them back home to kill. Depressive thoughts entered his mind regularly, and he considered suicide several times.

There is something to understand about Dahmer before we continue: he was not a psychotic case like many other killers. He was completely aware that killing was wrong and only truly enjoyed what came later—the defiling and dismemberment of their bodies.

Later, a neighbor stated that he had often seen Dahmer slipping into his own apartment guiltily—like a late-night thief—looking as if he was doing something wrong. Add the alcoholism and the fact Dahmer had shown strong signs of Asperger's syndrome since childhood, and it may be possible to understand him slightly better. His relationships never went further than a sexual encounter, and he was usually inept at getting to know strangers and forming bonds.

Dahmer was a rarity among young men his age, serial killers, and human beings in general.

Dahmer's social difficulties and obsession with paraphilias were never identified as part of a developmental disorder or mental health issue. Neither was it diagnosed or treated properly at any stage of his life. Dahmer, a confessed pedophile and secret serial killer, was as free as any other man, and he could do whatever he wished. That is, until someone detected and caught him.

That part of the story would take a while. In the meantime, unfortunately, Dahmer would take nine more lives. Despite the horrible acts our killer had already performed, the worst was yet to come.

Jeffrey Dahmer's horrific spree was about to reach its very pinnacle. The phase that everyone would remember him for was approaching.

Jeffrey Dahmer was about to die…

…and the alter-ego known as **The Milwaukee Cannibal** was about to take his place.

VIII

The Milwaukee Cannibal

IT WASN'T UNTIL FEBRUARY 1991—FEBRUARY 18, TO be exact—that Dahmer took his next life.

Cruising around the streets of Milwaukee, Dahmer came across seventeen-year-old Chris Straughter standing at a bus stop near Marquette University. He was an attractive model, which made it easy for Dahmer to entice him, using his most effective method: offering the chance to earn money by posing for nude photographs.

Curtis accepted. Halfway into their session of oral sex, Dahmer strangled the young man with a leather strap and began to dismember him. He had his Polaroid handy to record the whole procedure. Dahmer kept the victim's skull, hands, and genitals, as well as the photographs taken of each step of the dismemberment.

The next murder, however, would add an extremely gruesome detail to Dahmer's modus operandi. It will chill you to the bones.

As you may remember, Dahmer hated consensual intercourse because his partners moved and made noises, which he found distracting. Some psychologists believe Dahmer had always been in denial about his sexual orientation. They suggest this made him prefer silent, dead bodies that could not remind him he was having sex with a man.

For this very reason, Dahmer dreamed of creating "zombies." In his mind, these were creatures that had formerly been living men, but who Dahmer himself had transformed into mindless sex slaves, only living to serve his latest needs.

The focal point of Dahmer's first experiment involving this fantasy was Errol Lindsey, a mere nineteen-year-old.

Lindsey was heterosexual, but Dahmer manipulated him into visiting his house in exchange for cash. He became the first victim to go through the 'zombifying' process.

The chain of events started when Lindsey arrived at Dahmer's home. He was quickly drugged by the killer and did not open his eyes again until the ordeal was over. When he awoke from his long, sedated sleep, Lindsey felt weird. He informed Dahmer he was suffering from a headache and wanted to know the time.

Dahmer had used a drill to bore a hole into the man's skull. Then he injected hydrochloric acid into Lindsey's brain, in an attempt to permanently damage it. Dahmer felt insecure due to the victim's sudden awakening. He quickly sedated him again, then strangled and killed the youth before he could become a problem.

Dahmer decapitated the young man and kept his skull. He flayed the body and retained the skin in a saline solution. He would eventually have to dispose of it, reluctantly, when it became brittle.

On May 24, 1991, Dahmer met a man at a gay bar known as the "219 Club," which he had regularly used to find victims. His latest victim was an African-American named Tony Hughes, who was deaf and mute. At the bar, he communicated with Dahmer using writing and lip-reading. Dahmer lured the man home for sex and strangled him mercilessly, then carelessly leaving him to rot on his bedroom floor for the next three days.

However, just two days later, on May 26, 1991, a strange twist of fate took hold of Dahmer's life, bringing him the absolute closest to prison he had ever been thus far. First, it started when he met fourteen-year-old Konerack Sinthasomphone, who, due to coincidence or fate, was the younger brother of the boy whom Dahmer had been arrested for molesting in 1988.

He lured the boy to his home with an offer of money in exchange for taking some pictures of him in his underwear. Dahmer sedated Konerack using his trusty concoction and performed oral sex on the boy.

But more was to come.

As mentioned earlier in this chapter, Dahmer had always wondered about the possibility of creating "zombie slaves"—lovers who he could permanently take advantage of after putting them in a comatose state. He believed he could find a way to keep a man in a state between life and death, in which they could function at the most basic levels, responding to his every desire. His attempt to "brain damage" Tony Hughes had failed. Now he had another victim and was excited to experiment with this notion further.

Sinthasomphone would suffer the consequences of this curiosity that is obsessing Dahmer's mind. While the boy was sedated, the killer fetched a power drill, which he used to open a hole in the boy's skull near his frontal lobe. Not content with this terrible act, he began to pour hydrochloric acid into the hole in the youth's head, believing it would turn him into a mindless slave. The mix of acid and drugs made Konerack so detached from reality that even when Dahmer took him to his bedroom, right past Tony Hughes' body still laying there on the floor, the boy did not react.

Dahmer drank some beers as he lay beside the youth, studying the effects of what he had done to him. Eventually, he ran out of drinks and was forced to leave the apartment for a few hours. At some point, Konerack woke up...

...and escaped.

Konerack made his way through the apartment, cautiously at first, but soon found his way out of the building and wandered, dazed and nude, onto the streets of Milwaukee. Three women came across him shortly after. They approached to find the boy speaking in Laotian—a side-effect of the drugs, since Konerack spoke fluent English—and with no real idea of what was going on.

Unfortunately for Konerack, Dahmer was on his way back to his apartment when he spotted the scene and butted in, telling the women that Sinthasomphone was his lover and he had too much to drink and had gotten lost. The women did not allow Dahmer to take the young boy away. Instead, they called 911.

Two officers arrived quickly. Dahmer was suddenly in a very dangerous situation. Cornered, with two policemen about to go to his home, Jeffrey Dahmer had suddenly lost the upper hand.

IX

The Noose Tightens

THE TWO POLICE OFFICERS, JOHN BALCERZAK, who later would become the President of the Milwaukee Police Association, and Joseph Gabrish, arrived at the scene and intervened in what they immediately, and wrongly, concluded was an argument between two lovers.

Dahmer reinforced this opinion by convincingly stating the boy was actually nineteen-years-old, and often drank himself into such a state. Further, he added he had proof that would show young Sinthasomphone had willingly modeled for nude pictures. The three women were not as easily convinced. They told the officers to take a look at Konerack's buttocks, which were bleeding. The two law enforcement officers quickly shut down the women's requests. Instead, they escorted Dahmer back to his apartment, along with the now-covered, but still confused Konerack.

The walk back home was a nervy one, but Dahmer still acted as though things were under control. Once back at his apartment, he produced the Polaroids he had taken of Konerack, using them as proof the young man was with him consensually. The officers smelled something odd coming from Dahmer's bedroom, so one of them went to check it out. Dahmer must have felt great terror when the man entered the room where Tony Hughes's rotting body lay. However, the officer did not bother to do anything more than peeking his head around the corner.

The two men, now content with their search and not even having done a quick background check on Dahmer—which would have immediately revealed he was a convicted child molester—told the killer to take care of his lover and left his apartment. They even joked about it on their radio report. Dahmer finally breathed again, injecting his victim once more with hydrochloric acid to properly subdue him. This second injection was too much, and as a result, Konerack Sinthasomphone died.

Dahmer, content with having escaped an almost certain arrest, skipped work and spent the next day dismembering the two bodies. He preserved both victims' skulls in the freezer as trophies. He documented the dismemberment process and discarded the body parts.

A month later, on June 30, Dahmer met a twenty-year-old model, Matt Turner, at a bus station. He made use of his signature tactic that had served him so well: offering the model the opportunity for a professional photoshoot. It worked, and before long, Turner became Dahmer's fourteenth victim. In early July, Dahmer purchased a fifty-seven-gallon drum, which he filled with acid and used to dissolve Turner's body.

Five days later, Dahmer met twenty-three-year-old Jeremiah Weinberger, a Chicago resident. Jeff offered the man a chance to spend the weekend with him in Milwaukee, and after consulting with his roommate, Jeremiah accepted. They traveled together on a bus, arriving at Dahmer's home to have consensual sex and spend time together. Dahmer actually took a liking to Jeremiah, later stating the man was "exceptionally affectionate" and that "he'd been nice to be with." He didn't think of murdering him until Weinberger told Dahmer he wanted to go home.

As we have already learned, this was a trigger for Dahmer, who offered Weinberger a drink. The young man drank it, and once he was passed out, Dahmer drilled a hole in his skull. He injected boiling water in an attempt to turn him into a mindless slave, as he had with Sinthasomphone.

His plan half-worked: Weinberger fell into a coma and died two days later. Dahmer would remember this death—Jeremiah was his only victim to die with his eyes open. He placed Weinberger's torso in the fifty-seven-gallon drum to dissolve in acid.

On July 15, Oliver Lacy crossed Dahmer's path. He was an African-American bodybuilding enthusiast, who Dahmer enticed to his apartment in exchange for money and, again, the offer of a photoshoot. After they had sex, Dahmer quickly drugged and strangled the twenty-four-year-old, then having sex with his corpse. Dahmer decapitated and kept his head, heart, and skeleton. The latter formed part of a shrine he had begun to construct.

Four days later, on July 19, Dahmer was informed of his dismissal from his job. He had been absent from his position for too long. The killer did not take this well since his job had been the only constant in his life for the past few years.

Emotion took hold of Dahmer, and he went in search of another victim. Joseph Bradehoft, who was twenty-five years old and the father of three children, became his next victim. Dahmer strangled him and left him to rot on his bed for two days.

As it turned out, Joseph would be Jeffrey Dahmer's last victim.

Unfortunately for Dahmer, he had suddenly become sloppy, sloppy for a serial killer. Everything was about to come crashing down on him.

X

End of The Road

"I THINK IN SOME WAY I WANTED IT TO END, even if it meant my own destruction." ~ Jeffrey Dahmer

Jeffrey Dahmer finished decapitating and cleaning Bradehoft's body on July 21. By then, the man's head was covered in maggots, but he preserved it and placed it in his fridge. Then, he put the victim's torso in a drum full of acid. Dahmer decided to move on to his next victim quickly. Now that he was jobless, his life had changed. He had more time on his hands than before and less control over his urges. Things were going to get ugly, fast.

The very next day, Dahmer went in search of his next victim. He approached three men, offering them one hundred dollars to join him at his apartment. He told them he would take nude photographs of them, and then they'd drink beer and simply spend some time together. Only thirty-two-year-old Tracy Edwards agreed to join him, and the two went back to Dahmer's home. Once again, Dahmer's chosen victim was African-American, a fact that would later be given significance by those who tried to understand Dahmer's sick mindset.

As he entered Dahmer's apartment, the foul smells and sights immediately assaulted Edwards' senses. There were boxes of hydrochloric acid lying around. He suddenly felt very uncomfortable. When Edwards turned to look at Dahmer's fish, which the killer pointed out in an attempt to distract him, Dahmer moved quickly and handcuffed his wrist. He then unsuccessfully attempted to cuff Edward's wrists together. He took the thirty-two-year-old to his bedroom to take nude photographs. Edwards caught sight of the fifty-seven-gallon drum and identified it as a possible source of the ugly odor. He was no fool. It was obvious the strange man who had brought him to this apartment was disturbed in some way.

Edwards had no time to think of an escape plan; Dahmer pulled out a large kitchen knife and threatened to stab him if he didn't cooperate with the photography session. Edwards was quick to unbutton his shirt, attempting to calm Dahmer down—telling him he would do whatever Dahmer said. This seemed to work. Dahmer began to get distracted watching television as Edwards finished opening his shirt. In doing so, he was already looking for a way to get out of there and alert somebody—anybody—who could save him from this terrible situation.

Once Edwards was naked, Dahmer approached him and began to listen to his heart intently. He ran his knife along the victim's skin and told him he was going to consume the precious organ. Judging by what he had seen in the room, Edwards knew the stranger was not bluffing and that his life was going to be over very soon. He tried continuously to convince Dahmer that he was a friend, but the killer had already made his decision.

Edwards asked to use the bathroom, and Dahmer accepted, but the killer was waiting patiently when the victim stepped back out. Edwards knew he had to find the perfect moment.

And finally, five hours later, it came.

It was almost midnight. Edwards asked to use the bathroom a second time. This time, he noted a lapse in Dahmer's concentration. The killer, for all his caution, had not secured Edwards' handcuffs. Edwards knew it was time—he smashed his fist into Dahmer's face and kicked him in the stomach, knocking him off balance, running out of the apartment building and onto the streets, before Dahmer could make him pay for it.

Two police officers looked up, greeted by the strange sight of a man with a handcuff on one hand, and shouting at them. Eventually, they calmed him down long enough to get his story; a "weird dude" had lured him home and placed cuffs on him before threatening to kill him with a knife.

The officers agreed to accompany him back to the "weird dude's" apartment. They reached Apartment 213 and knocked on the door. A pleasant, thirty-one-year-old blond man opened the door and allowed them inside. He listened as Edwards recounted his accusation. Then he admitted that he had indeed placed the handcuffs on the man's wrist and offered to retrieve the key to free him from the device.

One of the officers told him to back off and went to Dahmer's bedroom himself, where he spotted the large knife Edwards had described. He also noticed an open drawer with pictures. On closer inspection, the officer saw Polaroids of bodies in different stages of dismemberment, and body parts in various arrangements. In a horrific realization, he noticed the decoration and background in the photos were identical to the ones around him. The police officer left the room and showed the pictures to his partner. Now Dahmer's calm demeanor disappeared; the demon was unmasked.

In an attack of desperation, Dahmer threw himself on to one of the officers attempting to resist arrest and avoid being cuffed. The two men managed to subdue him and place handcuffs around his wrists. One of them pinned him down while the other began searching the apartment for further evidence of what he had done. It did not take long—upon opening the fridge, Officer Rolf Mueller let out a loud scream, slammed the door shut, and yelled, 'There's a fucking head in the refrigerator!'

Dahmer looked up from the floor and knew it was over. The officer had seen the skull, and organs packed in plastic bags and glass jars.

With Dahmer's time finally coming, the guilt inside rose to the surface.

"For what I did, I should be dead," he said softly, just loud enough for the police officers to hear him over the sound of the second squad car approaching the building.

After the police had taken Dahmer away, a detailed search began within Apartment 213 of 924 North 25th Street. Police would find three more severed heads in the kitchen. Seven skulls, some spray-painted or covered in enamel, some bleached, were found in his bedroom. They found two human hearts swimming in blood at the bottom of Dahmer's fridge, along with an arm muscle on one of the shelves. Within his freezer, they discovered an entire torso, a bag of organs, and some flesh. While this was shocking enough, there were two entire skeletons hidden in a different part of his apartment and a pair of severed hands. Dahmer had stored two preserved penises alongside a scalp, and inside his fifty-seven-gallon drum were three partially-dissolved torsos.

To worsen the horror even further, police officers collected seventy-four Polaroid pictures from Dahmer's drawers, documenting the endless stages of more than a dozen dismemberments. Others showed his victims' corpses in provocative positions that were somewhat erotic. It was the worst kind of photography the police had ever encountered. Although these images would haunt their every dream, it was only through these very Polaroids that police were able to identify the victims.

Once at the police station, a detective named Patrick Kennedy questioned Dahmer. He would spend the subsequent weeks getting answers and details out of him. The killer believed that it was time to put an end to the horror he had created. He waived his right to an attorney. He admitted to having murdered sixteen young men in Wisconsin, and one in Ohio, in 1978. He confessed he had killed Steven Hicks due to his teenage fantasies. He disclosed that the man had tried to leave after sex and that had pushed his buttons the wrong way.

The confession led to an exhaustive investigation by the German Police, who wanted to make sure Dahmer had not killed anybody while serving the Army within their nation. Eventually, they corroborated that he had not.

When asked about the procedure he had used, Dahmer described how he strangled most of his victims after drugging them, while in some cases, he had injected their skulls with acid or boiling water. He told the police he frequently had sex with the corpses or masturbated on them, although this was optional.

Further, he described putting each body in erotic positions, typically with the chest thrusting outwards. The dismemberment, he explained, would follow soon after, and was often accompanied by a step-by-step documentation using Polaroids. Dahmer said he found cutting open his victim's torso and revealing the organs sexually arousing, especially when feeling the heat the dead body produced. He remembered every single procedure except for Steven Tuomi's. Dahmer said he was not sure how Tuomi had died; if he had been unconscious or not before the fatal beating. He did recall placing the torso over his bathtub to drain the blood, before removing the organs he did not want to keep.

Dahmer recounted how in disposing of the bodies, he experimented with various chemicals and acids—an attempt to find the best way to reduce the flesh and bone into a foul-smelling sludge. Then he could pour it down a drain or toilet. Dahmer confirmed retaining other parts he wished to consume or keep as trophies, and also admitted to having consumed the hearts, livers, biceps, and parts of thighs of several victims.

In his sick mind, Dahmer believed the victims could 'come alive again' within him. He even tenderized and seasoned the meat before eating them to give them an extra taste. Dahmer said that it gave him an erection to consume human flesh, although human blood was not to his liking.

Even after all of this horror, a shocking revelation was still to come. When asked why he kept so many bones, Dahmer revealed that he had been in the process of constructing an altar dedicated to many of his victims. He wanted to decorate it with the entire skeletons of some victims and the skulls of others. Dahmer believed the altar would allow him to "draw power" from his victims' bones. He admitted that, if there was an evil power in the world, then perhaps he had been heavily influenced by it, to commit these acts.

On the 25th of July 1991, Jeffrey Dahmer was charged with four counts of murder. The following month he was charged with another eleven murders. On September 17, he was charged with the murder of Steven Hicks, after the remains he had discarded in his childhood home's woodland backyard were found. He was not charged with the attempted murder of Tracy Edwards. He was not charged with the murder of Steven Tuomi, because he had no memory of this crime and no physical evidence was found.

On January 13, 1992, he pleaded guilty by reason of insanity to fifteen counts of murder.

By using an insanity defense, Dahmer was seeking an easy way to earn pity from the judge and jury.

It was not going to work that easily. Dahmer had committed too many evil acts. Things were not going to end well for him.

Justice was coming for Jeffrey Dahmer, just like it should have decades before. His tale was going to end as it began...

XI

Final Twist

TENSIONS WERE AT AN EXTREME HIGH. GIVEN
that the majority of Dahmer's victims had been African
American, there was a strong belief by the public that his murders
had been racially-motivated, so security measures had to be taken
around his trial.

The justice system installed an eight-foot barrier of bulletproof
glass in the courtroom to protect Dahmer, and heavy security
escorted him at all times. The fact that only one African American
person sat on the jury also increased the tension.

As for the killer himself, Dahmer's insanity plea turned an
already complicated case into a shit storm; to put things bluntly.

It added a new focus to the case of a man with 15 murder charges and was at the center of media attention. The media now asked: was Jeffrey Dahmer insane? How else could he have committed such horrific and inhuman acts against innocent victims?

The defense immediately began its battle to prove that Dahmer was, at the very least, suffering from a paraphilia; necrophilia, and his strong dependence on alcohol, and borderline personality disorder were powerful enough to drive his impulses and obsessions to an uncontrollable point.

Dahmer was also finally diagnosed with a psychotic disorder, a condition that would help the defense explain why he had committed acts so detached from human nature, such as cannibalism.

The prosecution was certain that Dahmer was not insane at all. He had all the signs of a calculating killer, who knew exactly what he wanted and worked towards his goal; submissive partners who served to satisfy his dark sexual desires and required nothing else from him. He was not a sadist either, instead simply using his victim's death as a vehicle for getting to his paraphilias of necrophilia and cannibalism.

The prosecution also argued that Dahmer had worked hard to find ways to lure his victims into solitude, where he could kill them easily and without detection, a fact that spoke of preparation and planning.

Dahmer's alcohol abuse was also pointed out repeatedly, with one forensic psychiatrist noting how the killer required a level of intoxication before he could kill. This fact, the prosecution argued, suggested that Dahmer was very uncomfortable with murder, and found the need to drown his inhibitions before being able to take a life.

Another expert said that Dahmer was killing gay victims because he hated them, just like he hated the homosexuality within himself. This expert also agreed that Dahmer was not insane, but instead extremely cunning, handsome, and able to manipulate a victim with ease.

On February 14, both counsels finished giving their final arguments, and the jury met to make a decision. While the decision was not unanimous, the majority dismissed the theory that Dahmer was not in control of his actions when he had committed his crimes.

The jury concluded the best place for Dahmer to end up was not a hospital, but a prison cell.

The court prepared to hear the verdict the very next day.

Dahmer was ruled to be sane and, above all, guilty of his crimes. He was sentenced to life imprisonment plus ten years for his first two counts of murder, while the remaining thirteen counts brought him a sentence of life imprisonment plus seventy years. If anything, he was lucky they would not execute him; the State of Wisconsin had abolished the death penalty one hundred and thirty-nine years prior.

As if the fifteen counts of murder were not enough, Dahmer was also tried not long after for the murder of Steven Hicks, this time in Ohio. The hearing was brief. Dahmer exited the court with a sixteenth and final term of life imprisonment on May 1, 1992.

Just to put this into perspective: Dahmer had been sentenced to a total of **nine hundred and fifty-seven years** in prison.

Dahmer said goodbye to his parents—who had been there at every stage of his trial—and was taken to the Columbia Correctional Institute in Portage, Wisconsin. There, for his own safety, he would remain in solitary confinement.

This procedure was implemented despite the fact that he made it clear on several occasions that he wished to be dead. He even told his mother he did not care if anyone attacked him. On one particular occasion, just two years later, a fellow prisoner attempted to slash Dahmer's throat with a makeshift weapon made out of a sharpened toothbrush, but it did not accomplish more than some superficial wounds on Dahmer's neck.

Dahmer slowly earned the trust of the guards and other prisoners and began spending more time with them. Prison authorities even assigned him janitorial work. He became comfortable. Part of him wanted to start over, so he found his way to the path of God and became a born-again Christian.

Even so, nobody wanted to see a man who had done what he had done becoming comfortable. In fact, there was one particular prisoner who wanted him dead more than any other. This prisoner was an African American, who had read about Dahmer's black killing spree. He believed that God had asked him to cleanse the evil from the world. And Dahmer was evil—no doubt about it.

The prisoner's name was Christopher Scarver.

Scarver had seen Dahmer in the mess hall and watched him playing with his food, pretending the pieces of chicken were body parts and the ketchup was blood. He had also found a newspaper reporting on Dahmer's crimes. He cut out the article so he could confront the killer and ask him why he had committed such horrible crimes.

He finally got that chance in 1994.

On the morning of November 28, 1994, Dahmer was assigned to work with Jesse Anderson and Christopher Scarver to clean the prison gym showers. They were all unshackled.

At one point, one of the two men poked Scarver in the back with a long object of some sort. This angered him, and he turned to see both men laughing at him under their breath. Dahmer then proceeded to clean elsewhere, giving Scarver the chance to follow him.

In Scarver's mind, his actions were justified because the guards knew he hated Dahmer and had still put them together, alone, in the same place at the same time. With no guards around to watch, Scarver felt this was tacit vindication for his plan, a sign. He was still carrying the newspaper article in his pocket.

Before confronting his prey, Scarver picked up a dumbbell from the weight room, ironically, the very same weapon Dahmer had chosen to kill his first victim, Hicks, in 1978.

Dahmer heard the man approaching from behind and turned around. He saw Scarver, with a piece of paper in one hand and a dumbbell in the other. Somehow, Dahmer knew what was coming.

Scarver described what followed in a recent interview:

"I asked him if he did those things 'cause I was fiercely disgusted. He was shocked. Yes, he was... He started looking for the door pretty quick. I blocked him."

With two swings of the weight, Scarver crushed Dahmer's skull.

"He ended up dead. I put his head down, Scarver said."

Not content with having rid the world of Jeffrey Dahmer, Christopher Scarver then went for Anderson and caved his skull in. Unlike Dahmer, Anderson suffered for two days before dying.

It was all over.

Jeffrey Dahmer—murderer of seventeen men, necrophiliac, child molester, and the man known as the Milwaukee Cannibal—was dead.

It would not bring any comfort to the families of the victims, nor would it make him any less famous to the public, but Dahmer was now gone from this world, unable to repent for what he had done or at least pay for his crimes.

The young boy who had been lost in the maelstrom at such a young age was now truly gone...

...forever.

Conclusion

"I SHOULD HAVE GONE TO COLLEGE AND GONE into real estate and got myself an aquarium, that's what I should have done." ~ Jeffrey Dahmer

The aftermath was huge. Dahmer had sent massive shockwaves through the lives of hundreds with his actions, and now they had to pick up the leftover pieces of their shattered world.

Dahmer's mother, Joyce Dahmer, asked the media if they were happy now that her son was dead. She also wanted to know if they were glad that he had been bludgeoned to death. She died of cancer in the year 2000, having attempted suicide on several occasions. Dahmer's brother, David, has since changed his name and lives in anonymity.

Lionel Dahmer grieved for his son for many years, even writing a book about his and his son's story. Proceeds from the book were sent to victims' families as compensation. He and his wife Shari live in Ohio.

Dahmer's assets were awarded to the families of his victims. His possessions were destroyed and buried in a landfill at an undisclosed location.

The Milwaukee community took part in a candlelight vigil on August 5, 1991, to share their feelings of pain and anger over Dahmer's murderous deeds. Over four hundred people attended in an excellent show of support for one another

The Oxford Apartments were demolished in November 1992. The land ended up as a vacant lot, after plans to convert it into a memorial garden failed.

In 2007, evidence surfaced that linked Dahmer to the murder of Adam Walsh in 1981. A police investigation followed. It was eventually declared Adam's father was correct in believing that another serial killer, named Ottis Toole, had been responsible. Toole had died in prison in 1996.

Tracy Edwards never recovered from his ordeal despite becoming a hero for his part in Dahmer's capture. He became homeless in 2002, after many encounters with the law involving drugs. In 2012, he was sentenced to eighteen months in prison after being involved in the murder of another homeless man.

As for Jeffrey Dahmer, his terrible tale lives on in the media, books, films, and television documentaries, which have continually studied both his mindset and motives. He was a unique killer with a strange sense of guilt hanging over him. Even as his crimes became increasingly heinous, he was aware that he was doing something evil but unable to stop.

In a way, many believe that he is not that different from the rest of us, in terms of his upbringing.

However, one can also argue that Dahmer's guilt over his actions and his awareness of reality may make him even more depraved than other killers. While many psychopaths experience a separation from reality and a lack of complete awareness of the damage they are doing to their victims, Dahmer was fully cognizant of the impact of his depraved behavior.

The case of Jeffrey Dahmer is proof that not all serial killers are the result of abuse and trauma. His story suggests that children must be properly supervised and helped along the road to becoming good, law-abiding adults.

Ted Bundy

The Horrific True Story Behind America's Most Wicked Serial Killer

Introduction

WHEN WE ARE CHILDREN, WE SPEND OUR TIME watching cartoons or reading tales that make an effort of stressing the great duality of good and evil, mostly in a clichéd manner. We learn to spot the good guys—those handsome people with friendly smiles and helpful manners; while the bad guys are always quick to grin, appear ambitious, and openly cruel human beings that regularly reveal their intentions early into the story.

However, in real life, things are often not this easy. History has taught us that some of the despicable, merciless, and bloodthirsty monsters have typically been those people who demonstrated the behavior that we falsely believed to be signs of *'goodness'*; purposely used to manipulate their victims and lull them into a false sense of security.

Ted Bundy was one such man—best-known for doing this, in fact—a killer who was as friendly as he was seductive. A heartless and remorseless murderer, Bundy overpowered and desecrated his victims' bodies—both before and after death. Their corpses were his playthings until they rotted and he had to dispose of them.

Quite possibly the most famous American serial killer alongside Jeffrey Dahmer, Bundy's name spread terror across the United States during the 1970s, while his killing and raping spree alone qualified this title, he can also claim two successful prison escapes that had women all around the nation terrified to go out at night.

Was he prolific? Yes, very much so—he confessed to killing well over thirty women, but it is believed that he killed many more. *Were his crimes widespread?* Scarily, yes. Women in up to seven states were his targets, and he would have gone on for longer if he had not been stopped.

Bundy was a natural-born killer who lived to cause pain, and you, the reader, are about to find out just how terrible the man was.

Ted, the main protagonist of our book, became known as The Campus Killer, as well as many other identities he adopted during his time evading law enforcement. This book will provide you with explicit details of his life and his killings. Murders, rapes, dismemberments, Bundy was a man who "did it all," and these events have been researched for your interest or disgust, depending on its relevancy.

As you will see, the ugly parts have not been toned down, nor is any of the gruesomeness that sensitive readers may have wished to avoid reading, been eliminated. So be warned…

…*The horror that was Ted Bundy is about to begin.*

I

The Birth of a Psychopath

EVERY MONSTER BORN INTO THE WORLD IS AN
innocent, screaming baby—Ted Bundy was no exception. On
November 24th, 1946, our killer was born Theodore Robert to
Louise Cowell in the city of Burlington, Vermont. In regards to his
father, nothing certain can be said—it has never been determined,
despite Louise claiming on the boy's birth certificate the father had
been a salesman and Air Force veteran. There were rumors among
the family that Louise's own dad may have fathered the child, but
no evidence was ever produced supporting this claim.

Whichever the case, Louise moved into her parent's house with
the newborn Ted, and lived in Samuel and Eleanor Powell's home

for three years. During this time, they began feeding Ted a lie—one he wouldn't know the truth of for many years—primarily due to social stigma and old-fashioned beliefs. The trio of adults agreed to make everyone believe Ted had been born to Samuel and Eleanor, and that his mother Louise was his older sister. These lies would go on until Ted reached his college years; the rage of being lied to for so long may have contributed to developing his psychopathic disorders.

Within the Powell household, Samuel was an abusive tyrant. In spite of initial claims that Ted had been close and looked up to the man, his family would later admit the grandparent had been extremely violent, bigoted, and regularly spoke to himself. Bullying at home was so powerful that Eleanor aged into a depressive, withdrawn, old woman who required periodical electroconvulsive therapy to treat her mental state.

Young Theodore watched this all through confused, infant eyes and it definitely affected him. At one point, he surrounded his aunt Julia with kitchen knives while she was sleeping. Then he stood by her with a grin until she awoke. While this is a disturbing behavior for any child, the fact that Ted was only three years old when it occurred, made it that more disturbing.

When Ted was four, Louise decided to move to Tacoma, Washington, where her cousins, Alan and Jane Scott, lived. This would be where Ted's young life would develop and his first run-ins with the law would occur; although they were minor offenses and showed no sign of a soon-to-be serial rapist and killer.

A year after the move to Washington, Louise met a hospital cook at church and they instantly fell for each other. The man, Johnny Culpepper Bundy, formally adopted Ted as his son, soon going on to have four children with Louise. Ted was always distant, feeling uncomfortable around Johnny and the children, and would state later that he had never liked him.

Ted's own recollections of his teenage life were memories of reading crime novels and magazines for stories and scenes that included sexual violence and maimed bodies, as well as peeping in women's bedroom windows. Ted's mother would claim he was an excellent son who never forgot a special occasion to gift her with something; he often spoke of his dream to be a policeman or a lawyer. Classmates also remembered Ted as a friendly, well-known student, yet Bundy claimed to biographers he had never grasped the concept of friendship.

Ted Bundy's behavior soon showed sociopathic signs and a general disregard for the law. Breaking into cars, Ted would steal objects he found inside with the intent of selling them. He was also quite skilled at shoplifting, taking advantage of it to support his skiing hobby. Ted was arrested, at least twice as a minor; however, the details of the incidents were expunged from his record as soon as he reached the age of eighteen.

Ted was done with high school by 1965 and began studying at the University of Puget Sound. He did not like it there because his classmates were all from wealthy backgrounds and it made him feel inferior. After a year, he transferred to the University of Washington, where he studied Chinese. At the same time, he looked for simple, minimum wage jobs; he never lasted longer than a few months at a time. Whether it was working as a grocery bagger, shelf-stocker, or volunteer at a Seattle suicide hotline, his superiors remembered him as an unreliable and untrustworthy young man. Ted also volunteered in political activities for the Republican Party, such as Nelson Rockefeller's presidential campaign of 1968.

It was around this time that Ted met the woman that would perhaps become the most pivotal of his life, even more so than any of his unfortunate victims. Although he had never been a model boy, things were about to turn a lot uglier in Ted's young life.

II

The Grudge

TED HAD A PROBLEM THAT HAD BEEN tormenting him all his life.

He always wanted to be just like those wealthy, happy young men he had studied with at both universities. Part of that was finding a beautiful girlfriend he could parade around, who would give him the support he craved. Ted finally found her in the spring of 1967, a beautiful young woman named Stephanie Brooks. She was pretty, rich, smart, and had a lot of class, just like the women he had observed longingly at university. Just like Ted, Stephanie studied at the University of Washington. She also loved him a lot.

Ted was truly happy around Stephanie; he envisioned a future where the two could be married and grow old together. However, while he was picturing these things, Stephanie was growing increasingly uncomfortable with her boyfriend's lack of ambition in life. He did not seem to be on a path to success. Her parents also appeared to dislike her partner, and this may have been an influence on the decision she took next.

When Stephanie told Ted of her decision to break up with him, he was in shock. It was a slap in the face for someone he had been trying so hard to impress, and find a way to be like the rich boys he envied. Despite many letters and attempts at recovering the relationship, Ted was unable to accomplish anything and it got to him. He entered a depressive stage, filled with rage and confusion, which led to dark thoughts.

Ted's heart was broken, and he began to harbor a deep hatred toward women—most of the victims whose lives he took were women that looked very similar to Stephanie: Caucasian, dark-haired, and beautiful.

It was around this time, in early 1969, that Bundy traveled east and visited several relatives in Arkansas and Philadelphia. He went in search of his origins and discovered birth records in Burlington,

Vermont, revealing the true details of his birth and parentage. This did not help his state of mind, furthering his anger toward the world.

He returned to Washington later that same year and met Elizabeth Kloepfer—known as Meg Anders in some documentation. She was a divorcée and single mother from Ogden, Utah, working as a secretary at the university. Elizabeth became Ted's next girlfriend, though he was not faithful to her. Ted's life was about to take a change for the better...at least for now.

Back in Washington, Ted felt he had a chance to try again and he re-enrolled at the university, this time studying Psychology. His grades were excellent; he also had a good relationship with his professors and became friends with many people in various positions. One of those people was a writer named Ann Rule. She would go on to write one of Bundy's most well-known biographies, *The Stranger Beside Me*. Even though Ann believed Ted to be a sadistic sociopath, she took somewhat of a human, defensive stance on him. During this time, Ted also became interested in fulfilling his childhood wish of studying law and began to think of a school where he could study to become a lawyer.

Describing Ted's sexual habits, Meg Anders stated Ted was insistent on practicing sadomasochistic sexual intercourse with her, almost strangling her to unconsciousness, on one occasion, despite her pleas for him to stop. He also requested she remain completely still when they had sex, not making a sound as if she was a corpse. Only in this manner could Ted reach orgasm.

Bundy graduated in 1972, and immediately joined Governor Daniel J. Evans' re-election campaign. He had started sending admission requests to begin his studies at several law schools, and some were considering giving him a chance. Ted stated that in his eyes, the law was the answer to his search for order. During his time working for Governor Evans, he followed Evans' opponent Albert Rosellini around, recording his speeches for analysis. Evans was successfully re-elected and Bundy caught the attention of Ross Davis, Chairman of the Washington State Republican Party. The chairman liked Ted and the way he worked and helped him with recommendations. These ended up helping Ted get accepted by both University of Puget Sound and University of Utah's law schools in early 1973, despite that he had not done well in the admission tests. He would decide on University of Puget Sound law school the following year.

Ted Bundy was on the rise. His success was spreading and he was showing signs of being a truly heroic citizen—on one occasion, he saved a three-year-old child from drowning and was rewarded with a medal by the city's police department. On another occasion, he was involved in performing a citizen's arrest on a thief who attempted to steal a person's bag. Bundy recovered the bag and gave it back to its rightful owner—an act that did not go unnoticed.

On a revisit to the University of Washington's campus, Ted came across his friends and professors; everyone had something positive to say about him. His newfound security and position in society were highly respected by his peers and teachers, and they now had a far different—and better—image of him than before.

Despite all the success and good news, Ted would get another chance to feel triumphant.

One of Ted's business trips in the summer of 1973 took him to California, where he met up with Stephanie Brooks; at this point, he was still in a relationship with Meg Anders. Stephanie was shocked by Ted's transformation—he had gone from a man with no ambition and little vision to a successful politician, graduate, and now a law student. He was everything she had wished for in a man, and this made her re-start their relationship once more, primarily due to the fact that she did not know he was already with somebody else. Stephanie flew to Seattle to stay with him a few times, and Bundy even introduced her to his boss, Ross Davis, as his fiancée. They discussed marriage during this period, and Brooks was over the moon.

But it was all for nothing.

In January 1974, only a few months later, Ted stopped answering her calls and ignored her letters. He did not visit her anymore, nor did he seem interested in continuing a relationship with her. When she finally got a hold of him a month later and asked him why he had distanced himself without any explanation, he told her he had no idea what she meant and hung up. She never heard from him again.

Ted had achieved vengeance for her earlier breakup, and proved that he could have been her husband; the husband she had always wanted.

Ted Bundy would not be satisfied with what he had done to get his revenge on Stephanie. For some reason, it just was not enough. Perhaps he should have just let it all go—acknowledge things do not always go the way one wants them to go, and had taught Stephanie a lesson for rejecting him. Perhaps his inferiority complex had come back with added poison and started to eat at him and fill him with doubts. Maybe Ted simply wanted to hurt someone for the bad things that had happened to him.

Ted was about to pursue a new career, one much darker than any previous.

The rapes and murders were about to begin, and once they began, nobody could stop them...

...Well, not until it was too late.

III

Something Finally Snaps

IT HAD BEEN A GOOD PERIOD FOR TED. ONE THAT had given him hope, showing him he was somebody worth a damn and could make a difference in the world. He had given his life a massive turn for the better, and rubbing shoulders with some pretty influential men and women.

Curiously, Ted's participation in the Republican Party would bring him close to Rosalynn Carter, President Jimmy Carter's wife, who in turn would have the strange misfortune of meeting John Wayne 'Killer Clown' Gacy, and James 'Jim' Warren Jones; both infamous killers who were as scary as the protagonist of this biography.

Ted was troubled and spiteful toward women, with a strong fetish toward hardcore pornography involving rape, torture, and snuff. Speculation was he had acquired the taste for it from his grandfather, Samuel, who was believed to collect pornographic material of extremely violent content. This would define Ted, in spite of doing well in other aspects of his life.

The exact date and location of Bundy's first murder have never been confirmed, due to the fact that he has provided biographers and investigators with many different and conflicting accounts of his acts during the period of his first murder.

To this day, details are still not clear. Ted once confessed to a member of his defense team, Polly Nelson, whose career would arguably be destroyed by defending the monster that was Ted Bundy that he first attempted to kidnap a victim in 1969, on a visit to Ocean City, New Jersey. He also told her he committed his first murder in 1971.

However, he also told a psychologist he had killed two women in 1969 in Atlantic City but also confessed to a homicide detective that he had first murdered in Seattle in 1972, before taking another life in Washington in 1973.

The facts were even more confusing when evidence was found linking Ted to the 1961 abduction and murder of an eight-year-old in Tacoma; when he was fourteen. He denied it.

The truth is that while Ted Bundy's official murder/rape records may have started in January 1974, with his first sexual assault and attempted murder, his taste for causing pain started slowly and with small but telling signs manifesting themselves a few years before then.

In 1972, a woman recalled having sex with him during a one-night stand, in which Ted choked her almost into unconsciousness until he reached orgasm. When she confronted him on why he had done it, he feigned ignorance. He confessed regularly practicing the same act on other women, and that it would help him enter a new state of mind, giving him great pleasure.

Shortly after this event, Bundy stalked an attractive woman at a bar and followed her into a dark alley. There, he found a large plank of wood and advanced past her, expecting the woman to pass through a secluded area where he would ambush her. Nevertheless, the plan failed when the woman entered a nearby home. This attempted assault whetted his appetite for a future attack. He began to stalk other women in the hopes of getting a chance to rape and murder them.

Ted's first true attack occurred when he approached one of his stalking victims undetected, to the point he was literally right behind her. He carried a club and his victim was distracted, opening the front door to her home. Pouncing on her, Ted smacked her with the club, causing her to fall to the ground and scream out; at the last minute, he had second thoughts and fled the scene.

Ted was learning, perfecting his abilities, and honing the necessary skills he would use in the future. He was very diligent about leaving as little incriminating evidence at a crime scene as possible, as well as beginning to find ways to earn the trust of his victims. Everything was a soft set of practice attacks, eventually leading to the big moment of his first sexual assault.

It took place on January 4th, 1974.

Karen Sparks was an eighteen-year-old dancer who studied at the University of Washington. She lived alone in a basement apartment in Washington and never could have imagined what was going to happen to her on that cold night: literally ruining her life.

Ted had been stalking Karen and realizing she was all alone, broke into her apartment shortly after midnight through a window without waking her, and found her asleep. What he did next was horrific—he wrenched a metal rod from Karen's bed frame and used it to bludgeon her unconscious, repeatedly slamming it on her skull without mercy. When she had been knocked senseless, he took the same bloody rod and shoved it up her vagina, brutally assaulting her with the rod, causing extensive internal damage. Leaving her for dead, Ted disappeared into the night, but Karen survived and was found lying in a pool of her blood the next day. She entered a coma that would last several months. She survived the ordeal, but with permanent brain damage.

Bundy did not wait long for his next attack, either—this new assault ended in the death of his victim. It left such a mark on his mind, Bundy needed a period of recuperation.

In the early morning hours of February 1st, Bundy targeted a similar victim to the previous one; Lynda Ann Healy, a beautiful twenty-one-year-old Psychology student at the University of Washington, who worked with special-needs children. She also worked at a local radio station giving ski reports. Lynda had actually attended psychology classes with Bundy. She did not live alone, sharing her cozy 5517 Northeast 12th street residence with four other women.

Unfortunately, this fact did nothing to stop what happened to her. Lynda slept in the basement, while her best friend slept in the room beside her. The other three women slept on the floors above; all of the girls were quite close to one another.

The night before the attack, Ellie—Lynda's best friend and roommate—thought she saw a shadow move past the window on the side of the house. Although it put her on edge, she thought nothing more of it after noticing how the strong wind was pulling at the tree branches outside. The truth would never be known. In all likelihood, it was Ted Bundy, already planning what would take place the next morning.

It was a swift, ruthless attack. In spite of the girls' security awareness, one of the house doors had been left unlocked. This costly error allowed Bundy entry into the house, and he descended to the basement. The noise of his victim could be muffled by walls and ceilings. Unfortunately, his crime was a complete success. Lynda did not even realize Bundy was in the room and suffered a heavy blow, knocking her out instantly. Bundy then gagged her and removed her nightgown, taking a moment to dress her in jeans, a white blouse, and shoes.

Never directly admitting to killing Lynda, Bundy only hinted at what he *would have done* if he had abducted her—but it is believed he took Lynda to his home and kept her there, continuously raping and hurting her until she either died or he decided to kill her. Meanwhile, back at Lynda's home, three of the girls had early classes or jobs and had already left.

Ellie awoke to the sound of the phone ringing. It was Lynda's boss, asking why Lynda had not shown up for her daily report. This seemed very strange to Ellie; Lynda had mentioned meeting an ex-boyfriend that weekend, but she was always responsible with her job and classes. Ultimately, Ellie decided to continue getting ready for class and, for a few hours, forgot about her roommate's strange disappearance.

By nightfall, the girls would learn more information—a missing person report had been filed and two officers had visited the home to check for any suspicious signs, without success. However, lifting Lynda's bedsheets, one of her roommates found a large stain of dried blood on the pillow and mattress. A careful search of the room also revealed: a bloodstained nightgown and the discovery of missing clothes. The details began to reveal a story about what had taken place; someone made their way into the house, attacked Lynda, and carried her off.

The police, accompanied by Lynda's roommates and friends, fanned out to search for Lynda across the city and surrounding areas, as well as to question neighbors for any eyewitnesses. Both the searches and the questionings yielded nothing, and the girls of 5517 Northeast 12th street slowly lost hope in finding her again. It would not be until 1975, when Lynda's skull was discovered in a wooded location west of Seattle, resting in the dirt alongside the remains of five other victims, that Lynda's fate was revealed.

At first, the abduction of Lynda Healy was not associated with the work of a serial killer, but as more women began to disappear in the area, the general climate of terror started to grow.

Unfortunately, Ted Bundy was just getting started.

IV

Unleash the Beast

THE BRUTAL RAPE OF YOUNG KAREN SPARKS AND the murder of Lynda Ann Healy set off something within Ted Bundy's mind that would be difficult to stop; it was a hunger that would never be satisfied and a thirst which would never be sated. The demon within Ted Bundy's heart was fully awake, and only death would bring it to heel.

The rumors soon began: a killer was out there—a man who hunted young female students, doing horrible things to them. Ted would become the scourge of the city of Washington, and labeled the Campus Killer.

238

But not yet, however. For now, Ted Bundy's name was not even whispered in the dark. He was still the nice, charming man who had majored in Psychology and begun law school. Bundy stopped attending entirely in 1974 and worked alongside some of the biggest Republicans in the business. Ted remained a nice guy— nobody ever imagining he could turn out to be one of the most despicable American serial killers to have ever lived.

At this point in time, Bundy was no longer interested in home invasions and killing his victims where they lived. His modus operandi was evolving—he found it easier and smarter to take his victims away from lonely areas on the streets of the city, where he would not have to worry about witnesses, spotting him breaking-in or leaving victims' homes.

It was in this manner that another woman disappeared on March 12th. Donna Gail Manson, a nineteen-year-old student at the Evergreen State College in Olympia, disappeared without a trace. She set off one night on foot to attend a campus jazz concert but never arrived.

A month later, two female students from the same campus reported the suspicious presence of a man wearing an arm sling, on one occasion, and on another occasion using crutches. He asked the girls for help putting a pile of books in his vehicle—a Volkswagen Beetle. Both attempts failed when the women became suspicious after he insisted that they enter the car. Ted quickly left. The arm sling and other similar tricks rapidly became Bundy's best bet at capturing his victims; he worked on their pity and generosity to lure them, and then they were his.

Unfortunately, Ted's trick worked on Biology student Susan Rancourt, who was heading back to her dorm from an advisers' meeting at Central Washington State College; now Central Washington University. Bundy savagely hit her with a blunt object, proceeding to kidnap, rape, and murder her, then discarding her body alongside Lynda Healy's on a wooded incline.

On May 6th, just three weeks later and two hundred and sixty miles away from his hometown, Ted Bundy murdered once more. Roberta Kathleen Parks, a student of Religious Studies at Oregon State University, left her dormitory to go have a coffee with her best friends in the nearby College Union Building. However, she never arrived at her destination. Bundy approached and lured Roberta into his car, quickly driving further from the college and terrifying her into doing whatever he wanted. Stopping in a secluded area, Ted raped Roberta, returning afterward to Seattle, raping her again before murdering her and discarding her body.

The abduction of Roberta really put law enforcement on edge. Both the King's County Sheriff's Office and the Seattle Police Department began to increase efforts to find links and evidence that could lead them to the killer. All of the young women shared certain characteristics; they were all young, white, attractive college students with long hair, typically brunette, and parted in the middle. Rewards were offered for any information on the missing women, and eyewitnesses were encouraged to come forward and provide their recollections.

May turned into June, and with it came yet another victim. Bundy was no fool; he had followed the terror in the media and the details of the police investigation taking place in an attempt to stop him. By now, he knew people were keeping an eye out for a man asking for help or otherwise approaching women on the street. Therefore, he decided to slightly change his modus operandi and sate his bloodlust with someone willingly becoming his victim, without the trouble of having to kidnap her. His next murder would differ significantly in the way it took place, and Ted confessed he enjoyed it a lot.

Brenda Ball, a beautiful twenty-three-year-old woman, went alone to the Flame Tavern in the working-class neighborhood of Burien, Washington. She told friends she was going to try getting a ride to Sun Lakes, on the east side of the state, to meet them later and hang out. Yet, after asking a band member for a ride to the club, she might not be so lucky. All alone and with no way to get out to the club, a man approached and began to speak with her. With a sling on his arm and a charming smile on his face, Ted offered to take her home but invited her to a party beforehand, for which she accepted. One thing led to another, and the two had consensual sex—with Bundy unsuccessfully attempting to satisfy his extreme desires. Sadly, not long after, the demon within him whispered enticing words and Ted Bundy acted. He served Brenda enough alcohol to knock her into a state of stupor, raped her, finally strangling her to death.

After Brenda was dead, Bundy kept her body in his apartment for several days, constantly switching her from his bed to his wardrobe and vice-versa. He stated he no longer felt the urgency of getting rid of the body since he was in a private place; he had taken Brenda there without worrying about eyewitnesses spotting suspicious behavior. While at his home, Brenda's body was bathed and make-up applied to her face, before Ted finally tired of it and decapitated her. Her skull and mandible were found in the area around Taylor Mountain, Seattle. Her body's location was never discovered.

Only two weeks later, on the night of June 11th, 1974, Bundy returned to abduct another University of Washington victim from the campus. This time, Georgeann Hawkins, a popular and friendly eighteen-year-old student, avid swimmer and one who loved posing in front of a camera, was Bundy's choice. Georgeann had just said goodbye to her boyfriend at his dorm and began walking back to her own sorority house. A few hundred feet of brightly-lit alley separating both places was enough for Bundy to strike. As soon as the worried call from the sorority sisters arrived at Georgeann's parents' home, they knew their daughter was in trouble. She had no reason to run away and her relationship with friends was healthy.

Georgeann's body was never found, despite detectives carefully combing the alley the next morning. Eyewitnesses who were questioned afterward recalled seeing a man with a plastered leg and crutches in the area, struggling to carry a briefcase. Additionally, they claimed a woman helped him carry the case to his car, a light brown Volkswagen Beetle. Though she had not realized it, Georgeann had been in the presence of a serial killer.

Bundy returned to work as if nothing happened. He had found a job at the Washington State Department of Emergency Services in Olympia. Curiously, this agency was involved in the search of the missing women. Working there helped him keep an eye on what information law enforcement was gathering. While there, he met Carole Ann Boone, a divorced mother of two that would begin a relationship with Bundy in the future.

When links from the cases began to crisscross and meet, news about Bundy's crimes spread like wildfire—six women of similar characteristics missing, while another had been beaten savagely and raped. The states of Washington and Oregon were terrified of the crime; young women stopped hitch-hiking, or going to bars or other night-time activities. Law enforcement agencies had a real problem on their hands; the killer was smart enough to avoid leaving any physical evidence behind from the abductions, and forthcoming eyewitnesses provided little in terms of useful information.

Nonetheless, a certain pattern was definitely evolving. A sequence of details began creating a level of confidence among law enforcement officers, raising the hopes they had a chance of narrowing down their suspects and perhaps even capturing the man behind all this craziness. The women were all assaulted or taken at night, typically around construction sites and around the time of mid-term or final exams. Further, at most scenes, eyewitnesses had spotted a man wearing a cast or sling, and driving a brown or tan Volkswagen Beetle. It was just a matter of looking for the car, or having officers at the right place at the right moment—surely it should not be so difficult to catch the killer.

But unfortunately, things would not go as planned for law enforcement or for anyone who had expected to stop Ted Bundy. Women were still disappearing.

If anything, Ted Bundy had only just begun his spree. Soon, the police learned how big a mistake it was to underestimate Theodore Bundy.

V

Excelling at the Game

ALTHOUGH HE WAS UNAWARE AT THE TIME, TED Bundy was about to conclude his killing spree in the Pacific Northwest. He was soon to leave the state of Washington for Utah, where he would receive an acceptance from the University of Utah's law school, and get a second chance at becoming a lawyer like he had dreamed of since childhood.

Having already abducted and killed half a dozen women, Ted did not want the number to remain at six. Six was too small a number for Ted—who had always been so ambitious and so indulging of his desires. He needed more.

Growing arrogant and full of himself, Ted's belief that he would not get caught, reflected what most serial killers end up thinking. He knew the police were after him and were just waiting for a moment to catch him at night. *So why not attack during the day?* It was a risk, but he was all about risks, putting effort into getting the prize at the end of it all. *Why stop at one victim in a single day? Why not two?* His next murders were going to be the most daring yet.

It was a bright, Sunday morning on June 14th, in the summer of 1974. Lake Sammamish's beach was crowded with families, and young men and women were bathing in the cool waters and enjoying a peaceful day. With an extremely hot morning and noon, a swim would definitely help out with lowering body temperatures and getting a beautiful tan while they were at it.

A group of young women was on the beach that day in their bathing suits—the feelings of summer joy in their hearts, taking in the sights, sounds, and smells of a lovely day…unaware a ruthless serial killer was observing them, while in a state of increasing agitation at the thought of finding a fresh victim. He was going to spill blood and fulfill his fantasies once more; it was only a matter of time, and Ted knew it.

At eleven-thirty in the morning, Ted Bundy headed out to the beach. He spotted Janice Graham, a blonde, twenty-two-year-old woman. A friendly voice spoke to her in a British or Canadian accent, saying a simple, "Hello." Before her stood a man in his mid-twenties, wearing a white tennis outfit, with his arm in a sling. He introduced himself as Ted and explained that he needed to load his sailboat on to his car, but was unable alone. He said this with a smile, pointing to his sling.

Janice felt awkward denying Ted help and followed him to the boat. They set off for the parking lot just off the beach. He spoke to her as they walked, making small talk and wincing in pain as he moved his arm. Janice did not find him suspicious in the slightest and had probably not heard of the previous disappearances; she answered his questions and revealed that she lived in the nearby city of Bellevue.

The conversation made their walk seem shorter, and before Janice knew it, she was standing by a metallic brown, 'newish-looking' Volkswagen Beetle. Her smile died and an alarm bell rang in her head. There was no sailboat, and the parking lot was emptier than the beach had been. When she asked what was going on, Ted dismissed her worries and told her the sailboat was nearby, up the road at his parent's house. All her pretenses of trusting and helping him ended at that moment and she conveniently remembered she had to meet her loved ones.

Ted reacted pleasantly to the rejection and let her go with a smile, soon returning to the beach to look for someone else who could help him. Janice would recall seeing him heading back in the direction of the parking lot and laughed at how *good* he was at what he did. Much later, she realized who she had interacted with.

Ironically, a second Janice enters this story; however, her fate not as fortunate as Janice Graham. Janice Ott was twenty-three, short, thin, and blonde, who, like Bundy himself, had studied psychology and worked as a probation officer in Seattle. She was a warm-hearted young woman who believed in helping those in need. She had a wonderful personality and was loved by her fellow co-workers and her husband of one year, who studied medicine in California. Janice Ott headed down to the beach on her own that day, grabbing her bike and leaving a note for her roommate she was going to spend a day tanning under the sun.

Bundy was standing just off the beach, watching all the girls— as a male eyewitness and DEA agent—would recall later. Ted seemingly discarded most of the women at the beach until he spotted Ott lying on the beach and walked toward her. He did not take long to repeat the same process he had used on the first Janice: asking her to help him load his sailboat on to his car. Janice Ott was certainly more flirtatious than Janice Graham had been and allowed him to sit beside her, introducing herself as Jan and asking him if she could get a ride in the sailboat later. Eyewitnesses saw her begin to gather her bag and pull her clothes on, standing with Bundy and walking off the beach in the direction of the parking lot. One of them, a female housewife, found Ted's behavior with the sling slightly off, believing it was all an act.

Bundy had been able to convince Janice Ott to leave with him.

Four hours passed, full of rape and torture. Janice Ott would be forced to endure the abuse in a nearby, secluded location. Ted did to her whatever he wanted, and the worst part is that he did not kill her when he was done. No. Bundy wanted to bring somebody else to the party, and he wanted Ott to be fully conscious and aware when he did.

So, around four in the afternoon, Ted went in search of a fresh victim.

A sixteen-year-old girl named Sindi Siebenham recalled being approached by a stranger in a sling. During the time that passed between Bundy successfully pulling Janice Ott from the beach and his return to the same place, he had lost his previous charm and calm manner. When he asked Sindi for help, she noted how his eyes were shifty and his expression was nervous—clearly, there was something behind his request for help that put her off and made her leave as quickly as possible, despite his intense insistence. Other women claimed he was hiding in the restroom and would emerge and attempt to convince them to follow him to his car.

He failed several times.

But then he had success. At just before five that afternoon, one of his attempts at capturing his second and last victim of the day worked. Poor Denise Naslund had no idea.

Denise, a nineteen-year-old computer programming student, went to the beach with her boyfriend, her dog, and two friends. After enjoying a picnic with a few beers and a joint to spice things up, Denise had a fight with her boyfriend. They argued over something meaningless, and Denise headed off to the restroom to calm down. Nobody stopped her, and this fact would probably haunt them forever.

A man with a sling had been walking back and forth under the shadow of the building where the restrooms were located, but nobody had become suspicious of him. Once Denise had finished

251

in the bathroom, an eyewitness saw her talking to the man, who seemingly approached her randomly. It was the last time she was ever seen alive.

When she did not return, Denise's boyfriend, friends, and family immediately knew that something had happened. Unfortunately, their intuitions were correct. Miss Naslund was tortured and raped, likely forced to watch as Janice Ott was killed before she herself was also murdered by Bundy. He knew he had been seen by many. He had made a big mistake, but still, he dealt with the corpses accordingly—decapitating them and discarding the skulls two miles east of Lake Sammamish State Park, not very far away from where he had killed them. The bodies were lost for good, yet nobody knew this.

Law enforcement and volunteers in the area decided to help search for the two missing women, some believing they had drowned and divers went to the bottom of the lake to search for any sign of either body. Others searched nearby forests and looked far and wide for any sign of them. Local sex offenders were brought in to police stations and questioned, but nothing came of it. There was disbelief—around forty thousand people had been in or around the Lake at the time of the abductions. How could the two women simply disappear off the face of the earth? Nobody wanted to accept there had been foul play involved. What type of deranged individual would be so bold as to kidnap in broad daylight, surrounded by a crowd?

Meanwhile, Ted arrived at the home of Elizabeth Kloepfer, or Meg Anders, who he had seen that morning and interrogated her to find out where she was going—primarily to make sure she had not been planning on visiting Lake Sammamish. Meg noted that the cold he had been suffering from for the past few days was worse than ever. When she asked what was wrong with him, he explained he had spent the day cleaning his car and helping his landlord, and it had made his symptoms worse. Still, he was hungry and wanted to eat some burgers at a downtown bowling alley. Meg accepted the invite to go with him and brought her daughter along. Later, she remembered how he ate as if he was famished, wolfing down two burgers and insisting on an ice cream. His behavior was strange and it made Meg feel uncomfortable, but she never said a word.

The days passed, and nobody managed to find anything that could lead them to these two missing women. A sketch of a man who witnesses had heard introduce himself as 'Ted' was released by the police and published in the Seattle Times the following week. The sketch was accompanied by a brief description that said the suspect drove a metallic Volkswagen.

Meg was at work when one of her colleagues chuckled out loud and asked her if the man did not look a bit like *her* Ted and even drove a Volkswagen to match. Meg laughed nervously but remembered how suspicious her partner had been on the day of the disappearances and how he had attacked her on a previous occasion when they were riding a raft down a river, and he had dumped her in the water, making no move to help her get back in the raft. She had seen something in his eyes that had terrified her.

Meg's mind began to fill with a terrible thought—wondering if perhaps she had gotten involved with a dangerous killer. She watched how a month passed and no positive news of the investigation was released. A five-thousand-dollar reward was offered for information, but even the best eyewitness accounts came to nothing. One claim of the man's British accent led police to believe that perhaps the kidnapper was a Canadian serial killer on the loose.

Meg decided it was time to call the hotline, which had been created to assist with the investigation, but a friend decided to speak for her. They called from a payphone and made sure to confirm if the Volkswagen in question was metallic and not dull like Ted's, and if its owner had been wearing a wristwatch at the time. Relief spread through Meg as the person on the other side of the phone responded that all reports had spoken of a metallic paint on the vehicle. Meg and her friend hung up before asking about the watch

Other people, too, recognized Ted as the most likely individual identified in the sketch, but after police did a quick search of his records for possible criminal records, concluded that a law student without any run-ins with the police could not be connected to the disappearances.

The weeks continued to pass, and Meg no longer felt as suspicious about her quiet, enigmatic boyfriend as she had been previously. She traveled to Salt Lake City to pick up her daughter and began to look for an apartment for Ted, who was going to transfer from his law school to the one at the University of Utah, after receiving an acceptance at the beginning of the month.

When she met Ted at the terminal, she was shocked to see he had cut his hair short and looked like a completely different person. In his mind, he knew there was a noose closing on him in Seattle, and he had to move away from all that heat.

He left Seattle for Utah on September 2nd. Not long after, people started realizing that the disappearances in the former city had stopped, and without linking it to Ted Bundy's departure from the city, they finally felt they could relax.

This was not the case, however. Five days later, two men were hunting on an old logging road a few miles away from Lake Sammamish, when one of them stepped on a human skeleton. He ran back to his jeep to bring the other man with him, and together with two teenagers who had been walking through the area, returned to find not only a skeleton but a hairless skull. Searching further, they found a clump of black hair, which belonged to Denise Naslund, and some strands of blonde hair, Janice Ott's, and a third skeleton missing its head, Georgeann Hawkins.

Six months later, forestry students would discover the skulls and mandibles of Lynda Ann Healy, Susan Rancourt, Roberta Kathleen Parks, and Brenda Ball on Taylor Mountain—another of the killer's personal graveyards.

These discoveries would chill the bones of local citizens for decades. The deathly mark that Ted Bundy left on Seattle would not disappear for many years, and even now, he is still remembered.

Now with Ted in Utah, it was the beginning of a new chapter of death and defilement.

VI

A New Chapter

TED BUNDY MAY HAVE BEEN SPENDING HIS TIME with Meg Anders, but he was by no means faithful to her—he was known to have been going out with at least a dozen other women. He began a completely new life in Utah, studying the law curriculum for the second time and preparing himself for another killing spree.

Something bothered him as he began his classes at this fresh house of studies; the level of difficulty had increased greatly and he found himself lost. It was a great disappointment to him. It was like a wall was crashing when he realized he could not start over and obtain a law degree with ease.

Bundy did not take long to begin his murders once more in this new city. In fact, it is believed that only nineteen days after killing the two women near Lake Sammamish and setting out toward Utah, he may have stopped in Vancouver, Washington, and murdered twenty-year-old hitchhiker Carol Valenzuela. Her corpse was found in a shallow grave along with another young victim named Martha Morrison, seventeen-years-old, both with signs of strangulation.

Police have never confirmed these murders, but the two suspects are Ted Bundy, and another killer named Warren Leslie Forrest.

Bundy also killed a hitchhiker in Idaho, raped and strangled. She is, to this day, still unidentified, and Bundy himself has offered mixed confessions about what he did to her corpse. He told one biographer he had disposed of the remains in a nearby river after doing his deeds, while he told Ann Rule that he returned the next day to photograph the woman's corpse and dismember it.

He then moved on to kidnap sixteen-year-old Nancy Wilcox, a cheerleader, on October 2nd in a suburb of Salt Lake City and dragged her into a wooded area where he raped her. Although he initially intended to release her—or so he would claim—she would not stop screaming, he was forced to strangle her. He buried her remains near Capitol Reef National Park. Neither were ever found.

On October 18th, Ted targeted Melissa Smith, the seventeen-year-old daughter of a local police chief. She had been heading to a slumber party when it had been canceled but decided not to waste a perfectly good Friday night and went instead to a pizza parlor with a friend. Upon leaving the place, she decided to hitchhike back home. There are mixed eyewitness reports of what happened next—some claim she got into a car and was taken away, others claim they saw her pass by their home before letting out a scream.

But the truth is that Bundy assaulted her with a crowbar, whacking her in the head so hard he knocked her unconscious. The blow fractured her skull and may have put her asleep for days—it is believed she was held for five days in Ted's apartment, while he satisfied his sexual urges with her.

Eventually, he grew tired of Melissa and wrapped one of his socks around her throat, pulling it tight until she died. Her body was found on a brush-covered hillside in Summit County, Utah. She was nude, and Bundy's navy-blue sock was still wrapped around her neck. She had been bathed, hair cleaned, nails painted, and makeup applied to her face. The dead girl had been cared for despite her abduction. This horrified investigators and everyone who found out later. Furthermore, the fact the killer had attacked the daughter of Chief Louis Smith made the public feel that nobody was safe and the boogeyman they had heard of in Washington State was now in Utah. Fear filled the community. No young woman was allowed to leave their home at night.

Still, there are always rebels. Even the strictest or more careful parents can always find themselves tricked or defeated by their children, who, in their innocence, know how to manipulate Mom and Dad to get what they want. It is exactly how the next girl became Bundy's victim.

The problem is, Bundy felt free once more. Free to hurt so many, as he had in Washington without the worry of an investigation breathing down his neck. He knew he was not a monstrosity, who stood out to the general public; his criminal record was squeaky clean. He was charming, handsome, successful, and women generally trusted his intentions. It was like being invisible to society, even when he was one of its greatest menaces.

Laura Ann Aime, seventeen-years-old, was one such girl who did not pay attention to the warnings of her parents. She was a free-spirited girl almost six-feet-tall, weighing one hundred forty pounds; if riding horses did not scare her, no rumors of a nighttime murderer would either. Laura's parents had taken the news seriously and told her not to hitchhike at night—this was the way the infamous killer was getting his victims. Laura, brave, and surrounded by the naive teenage foolishness of invincibility, told her mother she would take care of herself.

Laura was living with a friend, south of Salt Lake City. Since quitting school, she had been hanging out with undesirable company, and her parents were trying hard to put her back on the road to success and a good life. They called and visited her occasionally, trying to accomplish the change they so desired. Unfortunately, tragedy was about to strike their lives.

On October 31st, Laura left home and headed to a party in the suburbs of Orem, just ten miles north of her home. She enjoyed herself there but left just after midnight to return home. She was in the city of Lehi and would need to hitchhike down Highway 89 to return home. She started out with no fear anything could happen to her. What were the odds of coming across a serial killer on this cold night, so far away from his hunting ground?

Yet Bundy *was* there in the area, hunting for a girl just like Laura.

Since Laura and her parents only talked occasionally, when their first call went answered, they did not react. However, when a planned hunting trip with her father came and went and Laura did not show up, they knew something was wrong.

Indeed it was. Laura had been kept at Bundy's apartment; beaten, raped, and sodomized before he strangled her to death with a sock, just like Melissa Smith. Her body was found in American Fork Canyon on Thanksgiving Day of the same year.

Ted's next attack, however, would be different. It would signal Ted Bundy's first major mistake and the beginning of his downfall. Of this attack, much is known and little is speculation. Why? Surprisingly, Bundy's victim managed to escape alive. Undeniably, it was the very attack that would symbolize Ted's eventual demise, even though he would kill after.

Enter Carol DaRonch.

At around five in the afternoon, having been at a dentist appointment in the morning, eighteen-year-old Carol DaRonch left her home and set off in the direction of Fashion Place Mall to purchase a gift. As she passed the department store Sears, she was approached by a good-looking man with a neatly trimmed mustache and long hair. He identified himself as Officer Roseland

and asked her if she had a car in the parking lot. She answered she did, and he replied a suspect had been seen breaking into her car. He urged her to come with him to see if it had been damaged or to check if anything was missing. 'Officer Roseland' walked with long strides, and they arrived at the car within moments.

When they reached her Camaro, it was undamaged and seemed to be in the same state she had left it in. This seemed strange to Carol; however, she obeyed the officer's instruction to open the driver's door. When he instructed her to also open the passenger door, she refused, finding it unnecessary. He then asked her to follow him to locate his partner, who he claimed was holding the suspect. By now, it was around seven in the evening.

As the minutes passed with DaRonch accompanying him in his search, Bundy told her his partner and their suspect were probably at a police substation across from the mall; it was a building that actually served as a laundromat. She felt confused and suspicious but could not identify a definite sign that confirmed her suspicions—the officer was well-dressed, spoke well, and behaved professionally, just as any police officer would. After reaching the cleaners, he found the building's side door locked and told her to follow him around to his vehicle so they could go to the police station.

When she asked him for identification, the false officer laughed, flashed a badge, and put it away before getting into his Volkswagen. He locked the doors and drove, heading to a residential area.

Before Carol could ask him what was going on, Ted pulled the car over violently and attacked her, throwing a handcuff on to her right wrist. They struggled and she scratched his face, but he brandished the handcuff once more and placed it on...*the same wrist*. He was unaware that this action would save her. Carol threw her hand up to catch Bundy's wrist as he swung it toward her; a crowbar in his grip would have cracked open her skull, but she pushed it away. At that moment, she saw the perfect chance to escape; jumping out of the car and running down the street, disappearing in the darkness.

Bundy pounced out of the vehicle and considered following her for a moment, but it would almost certainly expose him to the neighbors in the nearby homes, so he got back in his car and sped away. He drove, feeling confused and angry, and, most importantly, defeated. Defeat did not make Ted Bundy weaker—it only gave him a stronger desire to succeed and satisfy his never-ending hunger and unquenchable thirst for blood, pain, and tears.

Where another killer may have returned home to lick his wounds, or at least take a night off to reflect on what had gone wrong, Theodore Bundy considered it a good idea to find a fresh victim; someone he could hurt like he had wanted to hurt Carol DaRonch. He drove nineteen miles north of Murray toward the city of Bountiful. A high school, Viewmont High, was hosting a musical, where he could easily find a victim fitting the typical characteristics he desired.

His victim was there. Seventeen-year-old student, Debra Jean Kent, was about to become Ted Bundy's latest toy.

Witnesses would recall seeing a stranger standing behind the auditorium, behaving strangely, and trying to conceal himself. He had also asked a teacher and a student to accompany him to the parking lot to identify a car, but neither of them agreed to follow him. However, it is believed at one point, he managed to lure the young Debra in the same manner and took her away. Not much is known of Debra's death or what Bundy did with her body—she was considered a missing person until only an hour before Bundy's execution. A single kneecap belonging to Debra was the only part found in the area where investigators and family members searched. Her family was torn apart by her death, as well as the grief of her brother dying at twenty-six in a car accident.

Elizabeth Kloepfer—Meg Anders—was alarmed when she read that young women were now disappearing in the Salt Lake City area; all but confirming Bundy was the man behind it. Without a moment's hesitation, she called the county police once more in November and was invited to the station for an interview by a detective.

By now, Ted was considered as one of the suspects in the disappearances, but witnesses had not been able to identify him in photos, probably due to his new look. Nothing came out of this interview with Meg. She called again a month later; a call which helped put Bundy's name on the list of prime suspects. Still, not enough evidence linked him to the murders other than descriptions of his car, and Bundy continued his activities.

Continued reports of murders and the current ongoing investigation near Salt Lake City, caused Bundy to push his murders elsewhere by 1975. On January 12th, he took his first Colorado victim. Her name was Caryn Eileen Campbell, a twenty-three-year-old short-haired nurse staying at a lodge called *Wildwood Inn*. As she walked down a hallway to her room after stepping out of the elevator, Bundy knocked her out cold with a crowbar and abducted her.

Despite the well-lit hallway and Bundy having to descend to the ground floor with a body, on his way to his car, he pulled it off, and was able to have his way with Caryn at a more private location. Her nude body was found buried in snow just outside the resort a month later. She had been cut with a sharp instrument and her head had been bludgeoned.

About a hundred miles northeast of this inn, a twenty-six-year-old ski instructor, who went by the name of Julie Cunningham, went missing as she walked to a date with her friend. Bundy's confession stated he approached the woman on crutches and asked her for help to get some gear into his car. He whacked Julie on the head with a club and handcuffed her, taking her to a remote location where he raped and strangled her. Bundy returned to Julie's remains six weeks later for unknown reasons; it is believed he saw his victims' corpses as trophies.

Bundy struck again on April 6th, 1975. His victim this time was Denise Lynn Oliverson, who had just had an argument with her husband and hopped on her bike to ride to her parents' home and cool down. She never made it. At some point along Route 50, she was intercepted by Bundy, who abducted and killed her. This murder was another credited to him only after his confession prior to execution, and Oliverson's body has never been located.

Ted cared little for the ages of the women he attacked, as long as they were pretty and could guarantee him sexual release. His next victim was only twelve; a junior high school student named Lynette Dawn Culver, who boarded a bus bound for Fort Hall. She was never seen again. Bundy would go on to claim he had abducted her and taken her to a room at the *Holiday Inn*, drowned her in the bathtub, and sexually assaulted her before disposing of the body in a river. Whether this is true or not, Lynette's body has never been found.

In May, Bundy became occupied with the visit of three co-workers, including Carole Anne Boone, who would go on to establish a serious relationship with him, as well as a one-week trip with Meg Anders to Seattle, where they discussed marriage. Meg did not mention the three times she had called the police or the interview she'd had with a detective, and Bundy kept his on-and-off relationship with Boone and a Utah law student secret, as well. It was a failing relationship that could barely be called a connection at all, but it would not last much longer.

June followed, and with it came fresh blood: Susan Curtis, a hazel-eyed fifteen-year-old who had traveled by bicycle to a youth conference at Brigham Young University in Provo, Utah. She attended a formal banquet with her friends and fellow students, before heading back to her dormitory to brush her teeth, as she wore braces. She was never seen again. She joined Nancy Wilcox, Debra Kent, Julie Cunningham, Lynette Culver, and Denise Oliverson in the list of bodies never recovered, despite Bundy offering the general location of their buried remains.

Two months later, Bundy claimed to have found God and became a member of the Church of Jesus Christ of Latter-day Saints. It is believed that he joined this faith due to the possibility of finding new, unsuspecting victims he could lure with false pretenses more than actually adopting religious beliefs. After his conviction, he received ex-communication by the church. When asked what religious affiliation he had, Bundy stated he was a Methodist.

Whatever was going through Ted's mind, there was pressure starting to build around him. Investigators, who were analyzing the murder spree in and around Washington State, had developed a database which allowed them to narrow down the names of people related to the victims in some way; classmates, acquaintances, owners named Ted, who had Volkswagens, sex offenders—as well as other important characteristics—and when they finally were able to get results from their archaic computer, only twenty-six names appeared on four of those lists.

Ted Bundy was one of those names. Meanwhile, the detectives, still stuck in a time when computers were not as reliable as they are in modern times, compiled a manual list that included similar characteristics that could narrow down the one hundred best suspects for the spree…

…Bundy was on that list, as well.

The problem was not just that Ted was part of those lists for the Northwest killing spree, either. It was the fact that he had moved to Utah, where similar crimes were now taking place.

Ted Bundy was now suspect number one on every list, and he would have to tread lightly.

He would try, of course, but as the old adage goes, *every swine will get his comeuppance*. Ted Bundy's life was about to become miserable.

VII

Unmasked

BUNDY WAS NEVER AN OVERLY-CONFIDENT killer in the way others are. Sure, he may have attacked in broad daylight on occasion or continued abducting and murdering women despite knowing there were strong investigations aimed at him, but he always did well to mask his true self and kept from revealing the demon within his heart—until he was safely behind a door.

Bundy managed to convince his political allies, peers, and professors that he was a normal—even bright and hard-working— human being, and women were charmed by him; after all, not all women he slept with were his victims. His mask was the most powerful thing he had; it managed to keep the police away. Experienced detectives were having strong doubts this law student, without any adult criminal history, was capable of hurting so many innocent females.

But the mask would fall off, naturally, as Bundy slipped up. Because every killer—or at least, *almost any killer*—slips up sooner or later. Luckily, in this case, it was due more to an observant police officer doing his job than Bundy actually making a mistake.

On the night of August 16th, 1975, Ted Bundy drove to the neighborhood of Granger, a Salt Lake City suburb and the second-largest city of Utah, in the hopes of finding a young woman to terrorize. He cruised around the area until the early hours of the morning, hoping to find a new victim. But someone else was also in the area—somebody who would end the killer's spree—at least for the time being.

An officer in a patrol car had been watching Bundy in his car, driving around suspiciously. Igniting his engine, he began following Ted. He recalled how Bundy sped up and fled the area as soon as he became aware of his pursuer, but it was too late.

The officer stopped Bundy and ordered him to open his passenger door. There he found a ski mask, another mask made from pantyhose, a crowbar, handcuffs, trash bags, a rope, an ice pick, a flashlight, and other suspicious objects. The officer immediately concluded that Bundy was a burglar, although the killer had explanations for why he was carrying each item.

Unfortunately for Ted, however, the officer had been following the case of the disappearing women and recalled how Carol DaRonch had described a similar vehicle belonging to the man who attacked her. He had also been informed that Elizabeth Kloepfer had reported her fears about Ted Bundy, owner of a tan Volkswagen, during a 1974 phone call, and these facts rang all of his alarm bells.

He arrested Bundy and a search of his apartment took place shortly thereafter; police found a guide to Colorado ski resorts belonging to the Wildwood Inn and a brochure advertising the play at the school where Bundy had kidnapped Debra Kent. Ironically enough, they did not search well enough to find the Polaroids of his victims.

Bundy was released due to a lack of evidence but was immediately placed under twenty-four-hour surveillance. Now it was just a matter of finding something that would stick and put him behind bars. Meg Anders was called, with detectives requesting an interview with her. Only now did the officers take heed of poor Meg's words.

Meg told the detectives how Ted had possessed many stolen objects and was always in debt. She also spoke of how he sometimes took her vehicle—also a Volkswagen Beetle—out at night instead of his, and he had not been with her on the nights the detectives found he had killed the Pacific Northwest victims, as well as the fateful Sunday when he had murdered Janice Ott and Denise Naslund.

All of the pieces began to fall in to place, and it was clear that Ted Bundy had been the murderer all along. Detectives moved to locate Ted's vehicle, but he had sold it to somebody just weeks before. It was located, impounded, and FBI technicians searched it, finding hairs identical to those of three victims.

To make matters worse for the increasingly desperate killer, Carol DaRonch was called in to view him in a lineup; amidst desperate sobs, she immediately identified him as the dreaded 'Officer Roseland,' who had attacked her so viciously after fooling her into trusting him. He was also picked out by witnesses around the auditorium at Viewmont High School, condemning him. As of yet, there was not enough evidence to link him with any murders, but Carol DaRonch's kidnapping and assault landed him criminal charges the police had wanted to pin on him since his arrest. He was bailed out by his parents for the sum of fifteen thousand dollars, but things had just begun to get ugly for Bundy.

Bundy was not just seen as the man who had attacked an innocent woman and possibly kidnapped and murdered another; he was strongly believed to be the culprit of over a dozen abductions and/or murders, and police were working their hardest to find any evidence that would help charge him with as many of them as possible. He moved in permanently with Elizabeth in Seattle—unaware that she was the reason the police were so sure he was the killer, and spent most of his time awaiting his indictment and trial. Surveillance became so intrusive that Kloepfer claimed that whenever she and Ted stepped out of the home to go out somewhere, so many cars started up that "It sounded like the beginning of the Indy 500."

A great meeting took place in November, where three investigators, one for each state where Bundy had murdered, met in Colorado and re-collected information with dozens of detectives and prosecutors from five states. The conclusion of the meeting left them with no doubt; Ted Bundy was the killer they were looking for and was just a matter of finding enough evidence to charge him with the murders.

His trial began February 23rd, 1976, Bundy accepting his attorney's advice of waiving his right to a jury; they both considered it would work against him, thanks to the media version of the crimes he was being accused of. Bundy was found guilty of kidnapping and assault a week later. Judge Stewart Hanson Jr. sentenced him to a minimum of one and a maximum of fifteen years in the Utah State Prison.

While imprisoned, Bundy was subject to a psychiatric evaluation. Doctors concluded that Bundy was neither psychotic nor suffered from substance addiction. He had no mental illness or lesions; in truth, he was of enviable mental health. An initial diagnosis of bipolar disorder was soon discarded, and experts concluded he was most likely an individual possessing a subtype of antisocial personality disorder (ASPD); basically and in layman's terms, Ted Bundy was a *sociopath* or *psychopath*. He was an expert manipulator that seemed to 'shift' from one persona to another, with one of Bundy's own aunts describing later how she had watched him turn in to a stranger on a dark night as they had stood waiting for a train. He had a lack of guilt or remorse that was characteristic of those diagnosed with similar disorders and evidence of narcissism and poor judgment that came with them.

But even while Ted was closely watched at the prison, and his mind was being studied like a test subject, Bundy was already planning his escape. In fact, it would only be four months after his initial incarceration before he actually made his first move.

In October, he was found hiding in some bushes with a kit that included road maps, airline schedules, and a social security card. He was apprehended and sent to solitary confinement for several weeks. Not long after, he was charged with the murder of Caryn Campbell, the nurse he had taken from the *Wildwood Inn* hallway. In January 1977, Bundy was transferred to Aspen.

After only a few months, what followed was an extreme mix of ineptitude and Bundy's own luck—the same luck that had gotten him this far. The killer was about to pull off something that would only be read in thriller stories or watched in movies—Theodore Bundy was about to escape in a most epic fashion.

His new trial, for the murder of Caryn Campbell, was a peculiar one. Ted lost faith in his legal team, viewing them as both inefficient and inept at their duties, or perhaps with an escape plan already forming in his head, Ted decided to serve as his own attorney—a legal right allowed to all citizens but further reinforced in this particular case because Ted Bundy was a law student.

Consequently, Ted was allowed to remain within the courtroom without handcuffs or leg shackles that would have been worn in any other trial situation, an obvious oversight which proved Bundy's natural ability to charm or generate trust within those he encountered. After all, nobody believed he was going to attempt to get away from the courtroom, much less escape the entire city and disappear into the mountains…

…but he did. Oh, yes…this heinous killer with no regard for another human life, knew what he had done. Bundy was not prepared to be locked in a cell, as more of his hidden graveyards were discovered. He could foresee his sentence slowly turning in to one of death. Bundy knew he needed to get away and soon, if he wished to remain free.

The question was just a matter of *when*? Well, *when* had finally come. On June 7th, 1977, when he was transported from Garfield County jail to Pitkin County Courthouse in Aspen.

Ted began the trial listening to opening statements, but due to the amount of paperwork he was going to face, he took advantage of a recess to ask for a chance to visit the courthouse's law library so he could research similar cases and attain any information that could aid in his defense. The request was granted, and Ted was allowed to enter the library with little surveillance.

He walked away from the entrance and began to move from bookshelf to bookshelf, appearing to look for something specific, but was trying to get both as far away from the guard escorting him and as close to one of the windows as possible.

At one point, having grown tired of the act, he disappeared behind a shelf and opened a window. Peering out, he could see the drop from the second floor he was on—it was no joke—to fall all that way down to the ground was risky, but in truth, he had no choice. *It was now or never.* Thus, setting in motion the decision he had all along—to escape.

A woman recalled seeing a man throw himself out the window and landing on the ground uncomfortably. Curiously, she asked a nearby police officer if this was normal behavior at the courthouse. In spite of the officer immediately sprinting in the direction she had seen Ted, the officer arrived too late. Ted had landed his jump badly, spraining his right ankle as he hit the ground, but adrenaline and desperation kept him upright and pushed him on, pulling off his outer layer of clothes to keep eyewitnesses guessing.

Law enforcement soon began to share the terrible news from one officer to the next: *Ted Bundy had escaped.* Roadblocks were set up all around town. Bundy crossed the city without a choice, having no vehicle to escape in, but went undetected and managed to disappear into the Aspen Mountains. He was wearing a t-shirt and shorts, making him look like just another tourist. Now outside the city limits, he had managed to free himself of the constant worry that the roadblocks brought him, but he had a new issue; he needed to find food, water, and shelter.

Now that he was already a fugitive, he did not have to worry about charm or his public image: all he needed was to take what he required and survive. On the mountain, he found a cabin. He broke into it and found food, clothing, and a rifle.

Bundy stayed at the cabin that night. When morning came, Bundy continued south toward a town named Crested Butte, but lost his way and began to wander aimlessly around the mountain. Two days of sleeplessness and pain followed. His sprained ankle was getting worse in the harsh cold, and Bundy knew he was in danger of being caught at any time.

With each passing day, Bundy was feeling increasingly weak. He decided to risk everything and go back to Aspen, where he could find a car and escape the area entirely. It was not the best plan, but it was the only one he had. This idea took him past the roadblocks and led him to narrowly miss search parties along the way. He found a car with the keys still in the ignition. Such luck was not only incredible but also extremely unlikely—it was as if Bundy had been blessed, somehow, though at the time, he did not feel that way.

Luck would not be enough. Two police officers spotted a car weaving from side to side as it drove along the streets of the city. They pulled the car over and finally came across the man they had been searching for over the past six days. He did not resist arrest. It was not long before he was back in Garfield County jail.

One escape had been incredible and unlikely enough. How would he be able to pull off another, especially with law enforcement making sure he never got the chance to make them look like fools again?

As the old saying goes, "never say never."

VIII

Unstoppable

ESCAPING PRISON WAS NOT JUST A DESIRE THAT any man stuck in a cage might feel; it was a need that drove Bundy crazy.

He knew how much he needed the outside world and what it brought him: women to unleash his fantasies upon, people to charm and earn the trust, and of course, the means to calm his massive ego, and a drive that had kept him going this far.

Theodore Bundy was not a man to be locked up in a cell.

Even so, many among his inner circle—as well as experts who studied the case—believed he was foolish and impatient for thinking of escape. His trial was falling to pieces. Most of the evidence found, the prosecutors had hoped to use against him, was inadmissible. It looked like Bundy was only going to serve the conviction on the DaRonch case—of which there were less than two years left. He had a strong chance of being a free man as soon as his conviction ended, and possibly avoid facing future trials because of his latest victory.

Bundy was obsessed with getting out, no matter what the cost. The fact his new partner and former co-worker, Carole Ann Boone, was smuggling cash into the prison for him and helping him plan his next escape did not help to deter him either. Carole wished to be near him, despite knowing what he had done—this would not change, even after it was clear he had killed dozens of women in the most heinous way. She would change her entire life for the man she loved so dearly. Other fans, men and women who deeply admired the killer, also pitched in with their own cash and respect, further fueling his deluded belief he was not doing anything wrong at all— that he was right.

Along with the cash he received from Boone, Bundy was also able to acquire a detailed floor plan of the jail, along with a hacksaw.

Allow me to break the fourth wall for a moment, reader, and inform you that what you are about to read is something you would have never imagined somebody doing outside of a movie. Ted Bundy was able to hide the hacksaw for weeks. Every night he took advantage of the noise his fellow prisoners made while showering, to saw a discreet square-shaped hole in the light fixture above his bed without detection. Something else to point out—there were steel bars in the ceiling, and yet he found a way to saw between them without anybody noticing.

Now it was just a case of being patient because Bundy had a problem to solve; he did not fit through the hole. Nobody seemed to wonder why Ted was losing so much weight. This diabolical killer was steadily eating less to shed the pounds to become thin enough to fit through the one-foot-by-one-foot square in his ceiling. The day did come, though, when he finally found himself thirty-five pounds thinner and able to pull himself up into the crawl space beyond the hole. Nobody saw him enter the space. One prisoner complained of movement in the ceiling of his cell, but his claim was ignored.

It was late 1977, and pre-trial motions had become tedious and seemingly endless. The prosecutor wished to link Bundy with missing girls in Utah, and the Aspen trial started to receive increased

284

attention nationally. Bundy wanted the trial moved, preferably to Denver, perhaps already having a plan around this new change. The trial judge granted one half of that request: the trial would be moved, but not to Denver. Colorado Springs was chosen, and it was noted how the judge had chosen a place where the juries were traditionally hostile toward suspected killers.

None of that would matter anyway, as Bundy had only been biding time for his grand escape just a few weeks later on December 30th.

The night was dark and quiet, with jail authorities allowing their staff to return home with their families for Christmas time, and many of the non-violent prisoners had been granted a brief leave—an attempt to alleviate the stress on the jail's budget. Bundy had practiced his escape enough by then and knew exactly where he would go after leaving his crawl space. It was risky—in fact, it was one of the riskiest places to go in the entire prison—Ted planned to emerge from the crawl space into the chief jailer's apartment.

And as incredibly insane as it may sound, the escape was a complete success.

At seven in the morning on December 31st, 1977, a prison guard walked past Bundy's cell and left him breakfast, thinking the prisoner lying in bed was still sleeping. The guard continued his task, moving away without a second thought. It was not until a few hours later when guards began to notice that Bundy had not been seen during the day that they ran to his cell and found the food tray still there, untouched, and decided to open his cell door.

What a surprise it must have been for them, when they pulled his blanket back and found only pillows and books underneath, and no sign of their prisoner—just the square-shaped edges of the hole he had cut in the ceiling above him. Bundy had simulated the shape of his sleeping body and climbed up into the crawlspace before wriggling his way to the section of the ceiling above the chief jailer's apartment. The owner of the room had been out that night celebrating with his wife—something Ted had probably already known, most likely from a source within the prison—Ted had undressed, put the jailer's clothes on, to literally walk out the front door of the prison without being challenged at all.

Bundy had then stolen a car and driven east before it broke down, and he was forced to request a ride from a passing driver. The person took him sixty miles east. It would be one of the rare people who had been in the same car as Bundy and survived to tell the tale. Ted soon found himself on a bus heading to Denver. There, he traveled to the airport and took a flight to Chicago. It was at this point, over fifteen hours later, that the aforementioned discovery of his escape was even noticed by the guards.

Laughable, or as silly as it all happened, the killer was on the loose once more, and he had decided to change his ways after being imprisoned. In fact, he was as bad as he had been before, if not worse, but he now had the added distinction of evading law enforcement. Gone was the impulsive desire that had gotten him so close to spending his life in prison; now, he wanted to turn over a new leaf. Ted was going to do things right, this time around.

Or actually, he was going to do wrong things much more efficiently than he had before.

Ted Bundy was going on one last spree that would cement his status as one of the—if not the most—fearsome serial killers in U.S. history.

IX

One Last Time

T ED NEVER BELIEVED HE WAS GOING TO BE
stopped.

He believed he was now probably the most wanted
man in the entire nation. Not only had he committed terrible,
heinous crimes across several states, but he had also escaped jail
twice and put law enforcement on maximum alert. He had followed
the investigation for years now and knew he could not allow himself
to be captured. The public was still divided in its opinion; some said
he was being framed for political reasons, but he was fully aware
that the people who mattered could put him away, or worse.

Once he had arrived in Chicago, the killer knew he had to keep moving. There were more distant places he could go that would put a larger distance between him and Colorado and the law enforcement along the way. He knew that traveling to the furthest extreme of the country was the most plausible idea at the time.

Bundy later confessed that he had briefly wanted to truly retire from his criminal activity if it meant staying out of prison. He resolved to begin working somewhere legitimate that could represent an entirely new start to his life. However, as soon as Ted was asked for identification on his first and only job application, he decided he did not really have a chance at finding a proper job or starting over. Ted Bundy returned to his old wanderings. Whether this is the truth from the killer's own lips, or simply one of Bundy's attempts to humanize his image and charm the court, as his final trials took place, we may never know.

His spree would end similarly to how it had begun in Washington—with the murder of young college students on a university campus.

Having escaped Garfield County jail in spectacular fashion and managing to advance toward Chicago without anybody on his tail, Ted began to cross states as he headed toward Florida. His first move was to travel to Michigan, by train, on the first days of January in 1978, where he stayed for around five days and lay low to avoid being recognized by eyewitnesses.

By now, he was on the FBI's Most Wanted list and had appeared in national news reports and papers, so it was no longer a game of local cat and mouse, which he had excelled at for years—it was more a case of being the sole objective of thousands of highly-focused police efforts—police under constant pressure to achieve results.

Once his time in Michigan had reached an end, the killer stole a car and drove to Atlanta. Then he ditched the ride and took a bus to Tallahassee, Florida, on January 8th. He was going under a new identity, Chris Hagen, and rented a room at a house near the campus of Florida State University.

It was around this time that his aforementioned job interview took place, but he quickly returned to looking for easier, less legitimate ways of finding money—he regularly shoplifted and pickpocketed women's credit cards to keep him going.

During this time, Bundy was already planning his next lethal attack on innocent women in the most obvious location, although nobody would have imagined that it would take place so soon after he had narrowly escaped justice.

The thing is, Florida State University possessed a sorority house that Bundy had been keeping an eye on since he had arrived at the boarding house he was living in. Chi Omega was home to a group of around forty young, beautiful women, who Ted watched hungrily, and waited for the perfect moment.

On the cold, dark night of January 15th, 1978, with a chilling temperature of twenty degrees Fahrenheit, Bundy crept up to the sorority house and slipped inside through a back door with a damaged lock, climbing the stairs with an oak firewood club he had picked up on the campus.

It was a few minutes before three in the morning, and twenty-one-year-old Margaret Bowman slept in her bed without a care in the world, after her friend Melanie Nelson had left the room only ten minutes before. She was unaware that Ted Bundy was standing above her with his hands wrapped around the log that would end her life.

The tall, slender woman did not even get to struggle as the object descended on her head repeatedly and broke her skull open, revealing her brain. Before she could even react, Ted pulled pantyhose around her neck and tugged as hard as he could, to the point where her neck became half its normal size and broke.

The saddest part of it all? *Nobody heard a thing.*

The rest of the women were still unaware as Bundy moved quietly to the next room. One of the girls found it somewhat strange that she had seen the hallway light switch off a few minutes earlier, but she did not know why it had happened. The killer stealthily entered the room of twenty-year-old Lisa Levy, admired her body for a moment before pouncing on her and beating her senseless with the club. The girl fell unconscious and Bundy began to ravage her; sticking a hair mist bottle in her rectum and then her vagina and pulling at her nipples so fiercely with his teeth that he practically tore one off.

In his arousal, he also bit down hard on her left buttock, leaving a mark that would be crucial in identifying him. When he finally concluded his assault, he strangled her mercilessly and left the room, believing she was dead. Lisa would die on the way to the hospital, suffering horrific agony in her last moments of life.

Kathy Kleiner, twenty-one, slept next door and was next to be brutally attacked. Kathy's jaw was broken, a pain that followed her for years, and her shoulder torn open. Karen Chandler, also twenty-one, was assaulted almost simultaneously. The oak log broke her jaw with such force that several teeth burst out of her mouth. Her left arm was shattered as she attempted to defend herself. Bundy ran from the sorority house once the women started making noise.

Only fifteen minutes had passed—fifteen minutes for Bundy to destroy the lives of four women and their families. Slowly, the unharmed girls began to wake up and leave their rooms to see what was going on. One particular girl entering the house after a date would recall seeing a man holding a club in his hand as he disappeared through the front door. She and another female student ran to where Karen was stumbling along the hallway and caught sight of Kathy crying hysterically, her hands coated in blood.

Lisa Levy was slowly regaining consciousness as she lay face down on her bed and blood pooled from her cracked skull. One of the girls, still confused as to what was going on, saw the girl's wounded nipple and believed there had been a shooting inside the sorority.

It was chaos, and the peaceful, fun lives of every girl in the house were shattered for months, years in the case of the worst victims. Even with this flurry of attacks, Ted Bundy was not over for that night. He wanted more, and he would not go very far to get it.

A few blocks away in an apartment building, twenty-one-year-old Cheryl Thomas, another Florida State University student, lived alone in a basement apartment. She was sleeping and never realized Bundy had broken into her apartment. He entered her room, bludgeoned her wildly with his club, fracturing her jaw and skull in several places, as well as dislocating her shoulder. Cheryl was left permanently deaf from the attack and dancing career ruined for good. He sexually assaulted her, leaving some of his semen on the bed, as well as two hairs stuck to the pantyhose used to strangle her.

Bundy escaped into the darkness, only then fully satisfied with the acts he had committed that night. The police arrived too late to catch him, but they found the evidence left behind, representing great progress in catching the killer.

Ted was unfazed by the media reaction to his attacks. He had spoken of being a changed man on his arrival to Florida, but he had not changed at all. He was still the same monster that had left Colorado. He proved this with his next and final attack.

A manhunt ensued, but Ted Bundy eluded police. On February 8th, less than a month after attacking the women on the

Florida State University campus, Ted stole a van belonging to the university and drove east to Jacksonville, where he cruised in search of a victim. He spotted fourteen-year-old Leslie Parmenter, daughter of the city's Chief of Detectives, standing in a parking lot and he approached her, identifying himself as a firefighter.

She may have become his next victim—one may never know—but her brother, who was close by, came to see what was happening and scared Bundy away from the scene. Frustrated, the killer left Jacksonville, heading to Lake City.

His next victim would be his final one, and possibly the one that revealed to the nation, and the world, that Ted Bundy was truly an evil individual, at least in the way that we use the term.

Kimberly Dianne Leach, a twelve-year-old, straight-A junior high school student, and dearly loved by friends and family, would never have imagined what was to become of her on the fateful afternoon of February 9th, 1978. Lake City had never worried about the presence of killers, rapists, or other dangerous criminals that hunted in mostly large capital cities. Those terrible crimes seemingly so distant and foreign to the small, close-knit community.

Kimberly is believed to have been approached by Bundy, who—according to the only unreliable witness, another young girl at the school—was driving a truck around the back of the school when the girl disappeared. Though Kimberly looked a bit older to some, she was still just a child. And yet, despite her tender age and innocence, Bundy had no sense of mercy toward Kimberly. She was taken to an undisclosed location where he raped and sodomized her, finally strangling her to death like many of his other innocent female victims.

Kimberly's parents were immediately alarmed when their little girl failed to return home, as she was definitely not the type of girl to stay out after school or to run away. She was reported missing almost immediately—a two-month search following. Sadly, her body would not be found until April 7th, 1978—seven weeks later—lying in an abandoned hog pen near Suwannee River State Park; the body was too mummified due to the dry weather to be identified. Beside her was a tennis shoe she had been wearing on the day of her disappearance. The news was a bittersweet discovery for the police, community, and her family.

As for Bundy, he had left Lake City for Tallahassee and eventually stole a car. Ironically, it was a Volkswagen Beetle. He left Tallahassee altogether on February 12th. When he ran out of cash and began to suspect that police were closing in on him, he wiped everything down in the room before he left and believed it was over.

For once, though, his sixth sense had failed him; he was not necessarily running *from* a trap, he was actually running *toward* one.

After midnight on February 15th, 1978, Bundy was driving toward the Alabama state line when he was spotted by Pensacola police officer David Lee, who spotted Bundy's Orange Volkswagen and found it to be a strange sight in a place he knew so well. The officer requested a *'Wants and Warrants'* check over his radio as he put his blue lights on to pull Bundy pull over.

The tag came back with the information that would finally end Ted Bundy's rampage.

The Volkswagen was stolen.

Ted immediately accelerated, knowing that something was about to go down. The chase continued for over a mile until Bundy seemingly gave up and pulled over at an intersection. Lee was cautious about drawing his revolver as he approached the driver's side, knowing he had no back-up approaching if anything went wrong. There was no way of seeing inside the vehicle either, and the patrolman was worried there was another person in the front seat beside the driver.

Bundy saw the police officer approaching and heard the order to get out of the car. He saw the gun, and studied the officer.

In his mind, a voice told him not to go down like this. *Fight. Escape, and you will be free.*

Ted got out of the vehicle, slowly, after the officer repeated his order. He lay down on the pavement and allowed David Lee to place the handcuff on his left wrist…

…then threw himself around to kick the officer's feet from under him, then throwing a punch at the patrolman a second later. They struggled, with punches flying in both directions, David's revolver pointed awkwardly to the sky as he fired a single shot to frighten Bundy, but it was useless. Ted pushed himself off the officer and ran, sprinting south and ignoring Lee's shout to halt. David Lee caught sight of Bundy's wrist, saw the handcuff, but believed it was a gun. It was all he needed.

Bang.

Ted fell, seemingly injured. Lee ran over to him and checked the man for a wound. There was none. Bundy got up, untouched, and fought to disarm him, screaming, "Help!" repeatedly in an attempt to get somebody to save him from this situation. It did not work—Lee finally subdued the suspect and took him to his car, reading him his rights and completing the arrest successfully.

As they both rode to the jail, and Bundy faced the reality that he was truly done, the entire nation knowing exactly what he was, he repeated, "I wish you had killed me."

The most ironic part? Officer David Lee had no idea who he had just captured.

X

Justice

IT WAS A LONG DRIVE TO JAIL, AND BUNDY KNEW It was over.

Interviewed by the policeman on duty, he gave his name as Kenneth Misner, although the police immediately discovered it was not true. When he was found, Bundy had in his possession: three sets of identification, including Mr. Misner's twenty-one stolen credit cards, a stolen television, stolen tags, and a bicycle, as well as the stolen orange Volkswagen Beetle.

Bundy had resisted arrest and assaulted a police officer—which the cops still believed was to avoid being arrested for theft, and not because he was a serial killer who had raped and ended the lives of dozens of women. However, it would not be long before they *did* know the truth.

Hours passed and Bundy collapsed—weeping openly and calling everybody he could to get any legal advice. Eventually, he informed the police holding him that he was Theodore Bundy.

Not long after, he called his longtime friend Ann Rule. Ann claimed he seemed distraught and desperate as if he wanted to confess everything to her. Ann had always felt that Ted had been behind the crimes after getting to know him at work. She offered to fly over to Florida, but the police soon stopped allowing Ted to make or receive calls, and she missed her chance.

Ted Bundy confessed many of his crimes during the long night of February 16th, 1978, and the general public was informed that Ted Bundy, murderer and rapist, had committed the crimes at Chi Omega Florida State University sorority house—as well as the sprees in Colorado, Utah, Idaho, and Washington—was finally in custody, and set to stand trial within a few months.

Bundy was held in jail while the evidence was studied, to see what would be admitted at his trial and what would not; most of the evidence at Kimberly Leach's crime scene and in the car that he had been using at the time was good but not substantive in terms of incriminating him. The bite on Lisa Levy's buttock was studied by dentists, and they concluded it belonged to Bundy.

More evidence arose before his June 1979 trial, and suddenly things were looking grim for the killer. Bundy had thought of using the insanity plea, but had followed another famous case, Son of Sam, and saw it did not work as intended. Therefore, he again decided on defending himself, in spite of court-appointed attorneys.

Those within the court felt Ted was sabotaging the trial with his egocentric, irregular behavior, even angering the judge on occasion. As all of this occurred, the nation watched intently; the trial was being covered by two hundred and fifty reporters and the first to be televised nationally in the United States.

A deal began to present itself for Ted, in which he would plead guilty to killing Levy and Bowman at the sorority house, and young Kimberly Leach after abducting her. In exchange, he would be given a seventy-five-year prison sentence, which was quite positive for both sides. Bundy knew he could easily receive Florida's death penalty due to the nature of his crimes. Talks advanced, and Bundy showed signs of accepting the deal, although his true intention was to file a motion after the conviction to dismiss the plea.

Then Ted changed his mind. Suddenly, everything did not make as much sense as it had. He realized he was going to have to stand in front of the cameras and admit his guilt to the entire nation and the world; it went against everything he believed.

A man with such an ego could not show the world how flawed he was or how vicious and evil he had been. Bundy decided to refuse the deal at the last moment and continued with his strategy of manipulating the trial himself.

It did not work.

Bundy was convicted on July 24th, 1979, for the murders of both Lisa Levy and Margaret Bowman, three counts of attempted first-degree murder for his attacks on Kathy Kleiner, Karen Chandler, and Cathy Thomas, and two counts of burglary.

For these crimes, Judge Edward Cowart sentenced him to two death penalties, and Bundy's plans fell to pieces once more.

Events only got worse for him as Ted was taken to trial again a few months later for the murder of Kimberly Leach, and found guilty once again. In a desperate attempt to save himself from the worst of it, before the judge began questioning Carole Anne Boone, Ted asked her to marry him and took advantage of a Florida law that stated, if she accepted, it would now constitute a legal marriage. Therefore, she could not be required to testify against him. She accepted. Still swallowing the lies that Bundy was innocent.

Carole gave birth to a daughter a year later in October and gave her his last name. Many wondered how this *'immaculate conception'* had taken place since conjugal visits were banned at the prison. It also shed light on the fact that inmates were bribing guards to allow them time with their partners.

Eventually, Carole would give up on Ted and divorce him. Many still blame her for being instrumental in his defense, when he deserved to sink on his own, unsupported.

Ted's behavior was different in the second trial, many noting he was regularly slouched in his chair, showed more of an empty glare, and erupted in angry fits he had kept hidden so well on previous occasions. It was here that he was sentenced to death by electrocution for the third time, the one that would eventually seat him in the chair.

His famous confessions—the ones that helped books like this one get written—came after this, at the precise moment he knew he was a dead man walking. Many of them made detectives and psychologists believe he had begun killing long before his first 'known' murder in 1974, and he famously claimed to have been heavily influenced by violent pornography—stating it was the source of many killers' obsessions and fantasies.

Slowly, each confession showed just how twisted Bundy's psyche was; he believed that many of his victims had been *'asking for it'*, with the way they *'radiated vulnerability'*, and showed amazement at the fact that people had even noticed him at the scenes of his abductions.

In his mind, nobody noticed anyone else, and he took it personally that people had positively identified him on various occasions. Again and again, he demonstrated to have truly distanced himself from humanity. Psychologists spoke of how he had created enormous barriers of denial that he used to contradict reality itself.

Execution dates came and went, as appeals from the killer attempted to change his fate, albeit unsuccessfully. Sometime during his time being held at Raiford Prison, it is claimed that Ted suffered an assault by multiple prisoners, who jumped him when the guards were not watching. The attack is believed to have been a gang rape, although this was not confirmed and the killer himself denied it. Further sources stated that a death row inmate would even shower alone, so it is unlikely any rape happened at all, much less one involving several men.

Hacksaws were found in his cell in the month of July 1984, and guards realized that a steel bar in the cell's windows had been sawed through and glued back together to avoid raising suspicion. The killer was moved to a different cell after this event.

Bundy's last stay of execution occurred January 17th, 1989. He could not appeal anymore or change anybody's mind—a date for his execution was finally set.

He would die on January 24th, 1989.

This decision finally unlocked the remaining shred of humanity within Bundy, although it is possible that he simply wanted to brag about what he had done. He began to give the details of his crimes and spoke of what he had done with the bodies.

Detectives were told he had kept body parts and belongings of the victims in his apartment, and had even used Meg Anders fireplace to burn a decapitated head. He had re-enacted scenes from detective magazines with several of the victims and had killed more women than those the police knew of. Over fifty was the number

Bundy offered—over one hundred was what many in the police field truly believed.

Bundy spent the last night of his life weeping in his cell, his old confidence now gone. Forty-two witnesses watched as he was moved into the death chamber and strapped to the chair, mumbling incoherently as he prepared for the moment he had sworn would never arrive.

"Do you have any last words?" Superintendent Tom Barton asked.

"Jim and Fred," the killer managed, his voice breaking. "I'd like you to give my love to my family and friends." Jim was his lawyer. Fred was the Methodist minister present. They both nodded solemnly.

The last preparations took place, and the electrode was fastened to Bundy's head. A moment later, two thousand volts of electricity flowed through the killer's body and his form lit up, while smoke rose from his right leg. The machine was turned off and a doctor approached.

He was declared dead at seven sixteen in the morning, as people danced, set off fireworks, and chanted outside the prison, *"Burn, Bundy, burn!"*

Justice was done. The world was rid of Ted Bundy.

Conclusion

"WHEN YOU FEEL THE LAST BIT OF BREATH leaving their body, you're looking into their eyes. A person in that situation is God!'—Ted Bundy

The notorious killer known as Ted Bundy died with many of the details of his murders still undisclosed, taking locations of many remains, and names of victims that the police never linked to him.

Ted Bundy was the original serial killer; the one that made police change their tactics and put young American women on alert, after a time when hitchhiking and helping strangers was the norm.

Bundy was not just another mad man with a mission—Ted was a revolutionary in the art of murder and the biggest name in

American serial killer history. He was not a sick maniac with a hundred traumatic reasons to be abnormal—he was, for all intents and purposes, a man with a normal life, who had succeeded for much of his youth.

For those reasons, Ted Bundy has become such an interesting killer to study. While there is no doubt that he was a dangerous, twisted individual who deserved what he got, he is still one of the entrancing cases of crime history ever witnessed thus far.

To his victims: may you rest in peace. You did not deserve to suffer.

To Ted: may the world learn from what you did so we may become better human beings.

To fans and readers: well…

Continue Your Exploration Into

The Murderous Minds

Excerpt From Mary Flora Bell

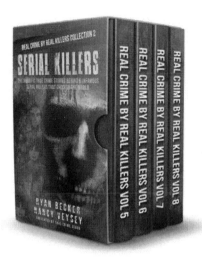

I

Meeting Mary

MOST AMERICANS ARE FAMILIAR WITH THE legend of the Bell witch, a tale that has spawned numerous books and movies. It centers around the haunting, and alleged murder, of the patriarch of a real family named Bell, who resided in Tennessee in the 1800s.

Supposedly, the vengeful spirit of a former neighbor, the witch, creates turmoil and wreaks havoc on the family in such a terrifying manner that it affected them the rest of their lives, and two hundred years later, the story is still being told.

One hundred and fifty years after the Bell family haunting, and an ocean away, a child with the last name Bell was making headlines. Her crimes would also traumatize the families of her victims for the rest of their lives. Called a witch, devil spawn, and bad seed, Mary Flora Bell will forever be the epitome of evil to some who hear her story and to those who lost a family member to her evil deeds.

Whereas the Bell witch was supposed to have the ability to shapeshift, it would be the English government that aided Mary to shapeshift and become invisible. Mary would be granted anonymity, as would the daughter she had years later, a controversial ruling. Although victims' families understood the need to protect her daughter, it was Mary's anonymity that was at the center of the debate.

Imagine, if you will, the horrific thought that a family member had been murdered, and you are notified that the killer will soon be released, but neither you nor anyone in the public will be privy to where they will be living after their release. Now, compound that thought by adding the fact that the convicted killer will also be given a new name and identity, which authorities refuse to reveal to you. How safe would you feel? When you stepped outdoors to check the mail, would you find yourself checking over your shoulder in fear?

As happens so often, the grief and anger that the victims' families felt did not resolve after Mary was locked away, nor did the terms of her release heal any wounds. If anything, knowing that she was going about her own daily life unnoticed and unidentified made the families of both her victims feel bitter, as though they themselves were prisoners. Mary was free to work and raise her daughter out of the glare of the media spotlight, but the families did not have this same luxury.

Mary Flora Bell—whomever and wherever she is today—will forever be known as the little girl with the angelic face who killed two small boys. In 1968, it was a crime which was quite unheard of, especially in her small corner of the world; Newcastle on Tyne, England.

It is a tale of sadness and brutality, as well as one of redemption. Mary Bell was a child damaged by the abuse she suffered at home and damaged by the lack of love and nurturing every child needs to grow and become a well-adjusted individual. Mary had been hurt so utterly deeply, that it seems pain was the only thing she had to give others.

The objective of this book is not to excuse any of Mary's actions. Even most small children understand right from wrong, but in Mary's case, it is difficult at times to discern whether she understood right from wrong and simply chose to do wrong, or if she was truly incapable of understanding the difference.

By studying Mary's psychosocial background, crimes, and the punishment she received, we can possibly gain a better insight into what went wrong, if the punishment was sufficient to meet the crimes, and if the punishment appears to have been effective.

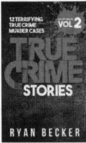

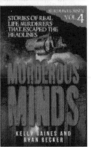
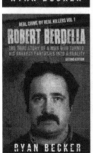
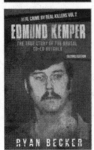

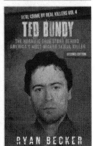

About True Crime Seven

True Crime Seven is about exploring the stories of the sinful minds in this world. From unknown murderers to well-known serial killers. It is our goal to create a place for true crime enthusiasts to satisfy their morbid curiosities while sparking new ones.

Our writers come from all walks of life but with one thing in common, and that is they are all true crime enthusiasts. You can learn more about them below:

Ryan Becker is a True Crime author who started his writing journey in late 2016. Like most of you, he loves to explore the process of how individuals turn their darkest fantasies into a reality. Ryan has always had a passion for storytelling. So, writing is the best output for him to combine his fascination with psychology and true crime. It is Ryan's goal for his readers to experience the full immersion with the dark reality of the world, just like how he used to in his younger days.

Nancy Alyssa Veysey is a writer and author of true crime books, including the bestselling, Mary Flora Bell: The Horrific True Story Behind an Innocent Girl Serial Killer. Her medical degree and work in the field of forensic psychology, along with postgraduate studies in criminal justice, criminology, and pre-law, allow her to bring a unique perspective to her writing.

Kurtis-Giles Veysey is a young writer who began his writing career in the fantasy genre. In late 2018, he parlayed his love and knowledge of history into writing nonfiction accounts of true crime stories that occurred in centuries past. Told from a historical perspective, Kurtis-Giles brings these victims and their killers back to life with vivid descriptions of these heinous crimes.

Kelly Gaines is a writer from Philadelphia. Her passion for storytelling began in childhood and carried into her college career. She received a B.A. in English from Saint Joseph's University in 2016, with a concentration in Writing Studies. Now part of the real world, Kelly enjoys comic books, history documentaries, and a good scary story. In her true-crime work, Kelly focuses on the motivations of the killers and backgrounds of the victims to draw a complete picture of each individual. She deeply enjoys writing for True Crime Seven and looks forward to bringing more spine-tingling tales to readers.

James Parker, the pen-name of a young writer from New Jersey, who started his writing journey with play-writing. He has always been fascinated with the psychology of murderers and how the media might play a role in their creation. James loves to constantly test out new styles and ideas in his writing so one day he can find something cool and unique to himself.

Brenda Brown is a writer and an illustrator-cartoonist. Her art can be found in books distributed both nationally and internationally. She has also written many books related to her graduate degree in psychology and her minor in history. Like many true crime enthusiasts, she loves exploring the minds of those who see the world as a playground for expressing the darker side of themselves—the side that people usually locked up and hid from scrutiny.

Genoveva Ortiz is a Los Angeles-based writer who began her career writing scary stories while still in college. After receiving a B.A. in English in 2018, she shifted her focus to nonfiction and the real-life horrors of crime and unsolved mysteries. Together with True Crime Seven, she is excited to further explore the world of true crime through a social justice perspective.

You can learn more about us and our writers at:

https://truecrimeseven.com/about/

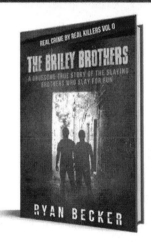

Dark Fantasies Turned Reality

Prepare yourself, we're not going to **hold back on details or cut out any of the gruesome truths...**

Made in the USA
Middletown, DE
26 September 2021